WOMEN
AND
MONEY

A Guide for the '90s

ANITA JONES-LEE

BARRON'S

All inquiries should be addressed to:

Barron's Educational Series, Inc.
250 Wireless Boulevard
Hauppauge, New York 11788

Library of Congress Catalog Card No. 91-16784

International Standard Book No. 0-8120-4546-7

Library of Congress Cataloging-in-Publication Data

Jones-Lee, Anita.
    Women and money : a guide for the '90s.
      p. cm.
    Includes index.
    ISBN 0-8120-4546-7
      1. Women--Finance, Personal. I. Title.
HG179. J578 1991   91-16784
332.024'042–dc20   CIP

PRINTED IN THE UNITED STATES OF AMERICA
234   5500   98765432

DEDICATION

For their support and nurturing, to

Fredric Lee

Mary Elizabeth Wilson

Theophia H. Lee and Philip F. Lee, and

Frances B. Harris

ABOUT THE AUTHOR

Anita Jones-Lee is a corporate finance attorney and a graduate of Harvard University (applied mathematics) and Harvard Law School with extensive experience in the fields of structured finance and securities. Her previous book on securities law and analysis, *Keys to Understanding Securities*, was published by Barron's in 1989.

ACKNOWLEDGMENTS

Like everyone who writes a book, I have ended up a debtor. I am indebted to the talented editorial staff of Barron's, and especially to Grace Freedson, the managing editor, for her belief in the project, to Jane O'Sullivan, for her keen eye and firm but gently put critiques of early drafts, and to Donna Jones, for her tireless attention to detail.

I am indebted to many librarians, but especially to the staffs of the New York Public Library and Harvard's Widener Library.

To the market researchers who opened their treasures to this stranger for no more compensation than the shared pleasure of finding an answer to a quirky question, I am indebted. Many institutions and organizations gave · extremely useful data for the asking. Notable among these are the Department of Commerce's Bureau of the Census, the New York Stock Exchange, the American Stock Exchange, the National Association of Securities Dealers, the Investment Company Institute, the American Council of Life Insurance, and the National Opinion Research Center.

Many friends and colleagues shared thoughts that improved the work. Of these, I am especially indebted to Darlene Eve Mason Denard and Fern Jones.

I am also deeply indebted to my husband, Fredric, though not for the usual reasons an author thanks family.

For my husband did not give up Saturdays, read early drafts, or even bring hot tea to encourage things along. What he did contribute was far more valuable. He simply believed in an unquestioning way that the work would be completed. And sometimes, when I doubted it myself, that assumption was indispensable.

I am most indebted to the women I interviewed, who somehow squeezed me into their living rooms and offices between tugging children and meetings. From you I learned so much about those moments when the truth about our lives with money transcends situation. These moments tended to be small, whispered rather than shouted. I will always be grateful to you for making me privy to your private truths.

                                                        a.j.l.

Contents

Introduction

The word "money," according to the philologist Bernhard Laum, stems from the Roman goddess Moneta. In Roman mythology "Moneta" is identical to the goddess Juno, who reigned over light, birth, women, and marriage, and in whose temple coins were struck. It seems the story of women and the story of money merged, at least symbolically, thousands of years ago.

But the story of women and money, or more precisely, the story of how money influences the lives of women, transcends symbol. Regardless of their financial status, both women and men, as the psychiatrist William Kaufman has observed, are "more or less continuously concerned—consciously or unconsciously—with the solution of their private money problems." And women have special needs that make the solution of such private money problems even more challenging.

This is a book about women and the solution of the lifelong, continuous concern that is money. It is a solution that will require that we as adult women give to ourselves the same patience we give our children, the same respect we give our parents, the same forgiveness we give our spouses. The solution will be as individual as that early project of drawing pictures with crayons, presenting as it did the choices of which colors to choose, the difficulty of making that perfect picture in our minds come true using clumsy not-so-perfect fingers, the same fingers which, try as we might, hope as we wish, sometimes color outside the lines.

Some of the explorations we undertake in the next dozen chapters indeed are way outside the lines. However, the basic theme, that women must make conscious choices about our total investment picture throughout our lives, suffuses this book. Making ourselves more conscious of the way in which money comes into our lives or slips out of it is not as easy a task as it might at first appear. Part of the difficulty stems from a reluctance of many women to acknowledge the complicated role money plays in our marriages, in our networks of family and friends, and in generally determining our lifepaths. The early chapters intend to help you look more bravely at money's everyday role as shaper of that lifepath. For most of us, our lifepaths and moneypaths are decidedly non-linear. And perhaps that should be expected. For few of us are fortunate enough to plot a straight-line investment course at age 20 and stick to it, never veering until retirement. No, most of us do not even get around to investing sensibly until we live a little, make a few mistakes, learn a few lessons, move on.

The book also was written because of the experiences of many women—and my personal experience as a corporate finance attorney—that so much of the useful financial literature has been written, and much of it continues to be written, in ways that assume the reader is male. These pieces are written for the general public, but subtly, and often unconsciously, exclude women as readers. One experience that comes to mind, and which is by no means the worst example of this type of language, is from an excellent text published in 1970 on interest. Each example of the concepts begins, "A man invests $400 in a mutual fund," or "If a man has $10,000, and he wishes to know..." These types of male-centric texts are, fortunately, fewer in number now than 20 years ago. Still, there are enough of them to make a book such as this one necessary if for no other reason than it lets women skip the mental gymnastics of becoming an abstract, generic "man" before tackling the financial concepts themselves.

Above all, this book is intended to be useful. The first third of the book explores some of the emotional challenges we face as we attempt to reconcile limited resources with the needs of family and friends, as well as with our own needs. We listen to the struggle of women to break free of financial roles imposed by their families, such as the role of the family's banker or the family's hero. We then show you how to reconcile the financial obligations implicit in the roles you choose to undertake—such as the daughterly obligation of caring for elderly parents—with the need to realize competing life goals.

The middle third collects in one place, in a "one-stop shopping" format, budgeting and savings techniques, strategies for reducing credit burdens, and ways to assess your risk profile and to establish allocation goals among investment choices.

And the final third introduces you to the basic array of investment choices and gives you a way to sift through the sometimes confusing jargon used to describe these products. You'll fine the analysis and language you'll need to ask appropriate questions of those trying to sell you these products, whether they be securities, real estate, tax strategies, insurance, retirement plans, or college savings plans. Here, we also review some of the storied swindles so that you can better arm yourself against fraud. In addition, the various theories of stock investing that have dominated the thinking of analysts for this century are surveyed. You may be surprised to learn you disagree with the basic theories your broker uses to invest your money.

In short, this book is a conversation with the women we are at those points where the lines become crooked and angular, sending us in different, unplanned directions. This book is intended to be a companion flexible enough for our travel in those unplanned directions, as we draw our lives way outside the lines.

a.j.l.

part one:

SELF-WORTH, NET WORTH

1. Special Risks

The failure to plan financially is one of the riskiest gambles a woman can take.

Though men and women alike face certain financial challenges—buying a home, providing for children, paying for adequate medical care, caring for elderly parents, and saving for retirement, to name a few—women are much more likely than men to suffer financial damage as a result of their failure to plan for these challenges. And, to make things trickier, women generally have less money to set aside to meet these challenges.

The Resources Gap: What Women Earn, What Women Own

Women continue to lag significantly behind men in earnings. According to the United States Census Bureau, in 1989, the median income for full-time employed women between the ages of 35 and 64 was $20,471, compared with $32,246 for men. And for those earning over $100,000, the gap between men and women widens even more: only 111,000 women earn at least six-figure incomes, compared with 1,303,000 men who earn yearly incomes above this traditional benchmark of affluence.

With less disposable income than men, women have a much harder time accumulating assets. A yearly income of $20,000 would place a woman above the so-called "poverty line," defined as approximately $12,500 for a family of four, but would not leave her much savings to increase her net worth over the course of her lifetime. Supporting this conclusion are data from a government population study, "Household Wealth and Asset Ownership." According to this study, single female householders between the ages of 35 and 54 have an average net worth—the value of all assets included in the study net of all liabilities—of $41,146, compared with an average net worth for men in the same age range of $53,981. Moreover, when you look at the allocation of assets women own, the picture is surprisingly unbalanced. Though over 48 percent of all women between the ages of 35 and 54 have regular checking accounts that pay no interest, *only 12.5 percent own any stocks or mutual fund shares and only 6 percent have money market fund accounts.*

The total value of assets owned, for the composite average woman across all age ranges, is as follows:

Cash in checking accounts	$ 544
Stocks and mutual fund shares	$ 4,157
Equity in home	$23,330
Interest-earning deposits	$ 9,457
Other interest-earning assets	$23,320

Women under the age of 35 own few or no stocks or assets other than home equity. Only 7.4 percent of women in this age range own stocks or mutual fund shares, and only 3.2 percent have money market fund accounts.

The significance of the earnings gap grows when you consider its effects over a lifetime. Let's look at an example. If a full-time working woman earning the median wage retires at age 65 after 40 years of uninterrupted employment, she would achieve lifetime gross (pre-tax) earnings of $818,840. A male worker earning his median would, over the same 40-year period, accumulate $1,289,840, for a difference of $471,000. And for a woman working part time (fewer than 35 hours per week and 50 weeks per year), the news is even bleaker: her median income before taxes is only $15,457 while the median income for a part-time male is $30,287, nearly double the amount. The comparable lifetime earnings of part-time workers over a 40-year career would be $618,280 for women, and over $1,211,480 for men, a whopping difference of $593,200.

What's behind the earnings gap? Why do women, after all these years of the women's movement, continue to earn only about two-thirds of a man's lifetime earnings?

Sociologists trying to explain the differences between what women and men earn have identified several possible causes, all of which play some part: that women leave the workforce more often than men because of pregnancy, childcare or eldercare; that women, in a small percentage of cases, choose not to work; that women are steered into lower-paying jobs that offer little or no chance for advancement; that women are denied opportunities to obtain higher-paying jobs because of overt or covert sexual discrimination; that even those women who gain entry to higher-paying jobs and who seem to be climbing the ladder with ease often crash headfirst into the glass ceiling of sexual discrimination and role expectations. But women caught in the earnings gap rightfully might ask, "What does it matter which agent is causing the earnings disparity?" They might rightfully point out to sociologists that a bullet fired unintentionally hurts just as much as one fired with malice. For regardless of the reason for the earnings gap, its effect on women is financially devastating.

And women face a double-whammy when it comes to making those lifetime dollars suffice. For not only do women have less money to deal with crises and challenges likely to deplete those earnings, but women also are more likely than men to encounter these challenges. It's as though men and women are two runners setting out to run the same course. But you put the female runner at a double disadvantage by first lining her track shoes with lead, and, to make matters worse, you give her more hurdles to jump before the finish line.

When You Become Your Mother's Mother

One extra hurdle women face is the care of aging parents. Women are far more likely than men to become the principal caretakers for elderly parents. In fact, studies show that over 75 percent of the caretakers for elderly parents are women. Caring for these elderly parents causes enormous financial strain. Since time is money, the financial strain often shows up first in the mounting hours used weekly to assist parents physically and emotionally. This time is shifted from time the daughter could otherwise spend at the workplace. Shaving minutes from workday mornings to ferry parents to doctors' appointments, dressing and sometimes bathing parents who can no longer do for themselves, and constantly calling during the day "just to check" have turned these daughters into double parents. And though for some, nursing homes can be used to shoulder some of this burden, for many others nursing homes are, both financially and emotionally, beyond their means.

So it is the adult daughter who steps in to care for these elderly. Interestingly, the phenomenon of double-parenting is not limited to blood ties, as women also appear to be taking on the care of their parents-in-law in increasing numbers. Parenting the generation below her and the one above her, these daughters and daughters-in-law are coming to be known as the "sandwiched" generation.

Listen to the struggle of Jacqueline, a 67-year-old retired secretary:

"It feels as though as I've always been somebody's mamma," laughs Jackie. Jackie is the laughing, never complaining mother of three girls and two boys, all now grown. At age 49, when Jackie felt her child-raising was over, her then 69-year-old mother had a stroke, which left her incapacitated, and Jackie found she had to take on the full-time job of being her mother's mother. Before her mother's stroke, Jackie dreamed of taking a once-in-a-lifetime cruise to the Caribbean. Now, she sits by her mother's bed, stroking the older woman's gray hair, and reading a magazine about the Caribbean. Jackie's hair is nearly all gray itself, and one cannot help wondering, "Who will be stroking Jackie's head when the time comes?"

When asked whether she'll take that trip someday, Jackie laughs: "I can't think of all that." But when Jackie's laughter ends, there remains an echo of bitterness.

Along with housekeeping duties—which can be doubled—the sandwiched daughter often assumes responsibility for managing the financial affairs of her elderly parent as well as her own budget. In effect, she becomes a surrogate worrier. She is the one who must deal with processing the hospital bills through the labyrinthine medical insurance system. If the Social Security check is delayed or arrives bearing the wrong amount, she follows up phone calls with letters with more phone calls and so on. The day-to-day emotional strain drains resourcefulness and energy she could otherwise use producing income. In addition, often the fixed incomes of the elderly don't cover their total expenses. What fills the gap? The pocketbook of the sandwiched daughter. Ironically, the sandwiched daughter finds herself in the position of needing more income to fund eldercare but, because of the time she must spend providing eldercare, having less and less time to earn it. To paraphrase the words of one woman caught in this kind of irony, the pace of her days becomes "like a merry-go-round" that she can't jump off.

Double-parenting exacts a heavy toll on women's careers. A human resources executive of a Fortune 500 company talked about how the struggle to juggle demands of eldercare with inflexible work hours has forced many talented women from the workforce. "These women become masters of the art of splitting time finer and finer. I can't tell you the number of women who've sat in my office giving me their resignations simply because they couldn't split themselves up any finer." Caregiving clearly has its costs. Though quantifying the dollar costs of eldercare is difficult, it can safely be assumed that on average the sandwiched

woman must devote at least one hour per day to performing tasks directly or indirectly related to eldercare. If we
convert this to an hourly rate of $10 (assuming the median
annual salary of $20,000), and assume she could otherwise
spend the time working, the dollar value of time spent in
eldercare would be $3,600 annually. And in all likelihood,
the one-hour estimate is too conservative. If we make the
more realistic assumption that she devotes two hours a day
to eldercare, the dollars spent for such care would be
$7,200, an enormous amount when you consider that the
median annual salary is only $20,000.

Outliving Your Retirement Dollars

Another financial hurdle more challenging for women
than men to overcome is funding retirement. It has been
estimated that most Americans will need an income equal
to at least 70 percent of their peak annual working income
for each year of retirement. Studies also predict that
Americans planning for retirement today cannot count on
the same amount of support from the Social Security system, which made up so much of the retirement nest-eggs
for past generations. According to research conducted by
the American Council of Life Insurance, 70 percent of
women surveyed do not have confidence in Social
Security's future. Men are more sanguine, with 57 percent
expressing doubts that Social Security will be there when
they need it.

But despite the critical need to plan for retirement, studies also show that most Americans are saving inadequately
to fund retirement. Women, especially, are at risk for outliving their retirement dollars. According to the latest
data on longevity, after age 65 women live an average
of twelve years longer than men. For this reason, women
need a much longer retirement income stream than
men. For even if men and women had nest-eggs of
equal size, women are much more likely than men to
run out of retirement money before death. And remember,
women must produce this extra twelve years of income

from lifetime earnings that average only about two-thirds of what men earn.

The prospect of outliving retirement savings has many of us worried. Women are much more concerned than men that their retirement savings will not be enough. Sixty-seven percent of women surveyed by the American Council of Life Insurance are concerned that their savings for retirement will run out. To create a longer retirement income stream, women must plan especially well, and such planning will involve an array of investments.

When Your Marriage Falls Apart

Another event likely to damage women financially more than men is divorce. Without a doubt, for both men and women, divorce is a trauma to the pocketbook as well as the mind. But, here again, the financial impact is much deeper for women. Studies show that women become much "poorer" than men following divorce. That is, if we measure "poor" by the poverty line, these studies show that women are more likely than men to slip below the poverty line after divorce, and the period during which they remain poor is longer than men. This is true, it turns out, for women who are viewed as middleclass or upper middle-class before divorce as well as for those women who were poor before divorce. This reality contrasts sharply with the stereotype of the "gold digging" woman who increases her net worth with each successive divorce.

Part of the reason divorce can deal such a serious financial blow is that women continue to remain custodial parents in the overwhelming number of cases following divorce. In 1981, the latest year for which data is available, 59 percent of divorced and separated mothers were awarded custody of children following the break-up of the marriage. But only 48 percent of divorced or separated women were scheduled to receive child support payments during the year. Only 35 percent actually received any payments at all. Only 23 percent received the full amount awarded. And even in the relatively small number of cases in which the woman receives the full amount of child support awarded, the payments often do not cover the actual costs of child care. Some of these costs are "soft" costs, which are hard to measure but nonetheless damage a woman's budget. For example, the need to ferry children to school sometimes delays the start of the workday, a delay which, for women paid hourly, directly translates into lost dollars.

Numerous studies have demonstrated that women experience a marked drop in their standard of living following divorce. One such study, of a group of women living in Los Angeles, showed that following divorce, men reported a 42 percent improvement in their standard of living, *while women reported a 73 percent drop.*

Many women try to make critical financial decisions during the time when they also are trying to cope with the emotional stress of divorce. Yet the financial decisions made during divorce will affect their lives for years to come. I recall a friend who went through a particularly brutal divorce in 1987. Her husband was an educator whose income barely approached half hers, and he believed her family was wealthy. When she filed for divorce, he decided to, in his words, "bleed her dry." Many thousands of dollars of legal fees later, she had had enough. "I'd give him anything I have," she said, "if he'd just get out of my life." The massive emotional strain of divorce had overwhelmed her ability to make sound financial decisions.

Eight Out of Ten Married Women Will One Day Be Widows

An overwhelming number of married women will one day be widows. According to Census Bureau projections, almost eight out of every ten women married today can expect to be widows. As of 1990, this country had over 11 million widows. In an insightful piece by Carol Lawson in *The New York Times,* entitled "Try to Tell a Widow that Life Goes On," we see the successful comedienne and talk show host Joan Rivers trying to cope with the loss of her husband, Edgar, from suicide. Trying to take on her own financial management, she was alarmed that, "I didn't even know the name of my bank."

The emotional paralysis some widows face is hard to overstate. Following the death of her husband of thirty years, my elderly aunt refuses to remove his name from the telephone listings, though he died over ten years ago.

During the aftershock of divorce or widowhood, the watchword is *caution*. If you do not already have a financial and legal team in place before these crises, then postpone major investment decisions for six months or so following the shock. An even longer recuperative period may be needed for some. Be wary also of any financial presences in your life during the recuperative period. Some unscrupulous companies review probate notices, obituaries, or other sources to identify new widows in order to sell investment products.

Hidden Discrimination: Women Are Charged More for Some Products

Yet another special financial risk women face stems from outright sexual discrimination. We have briefly touched upon the discrimination that steers women into lower-paying jobs or makes them collide headfirst with corporate glass ceilings. Another largely unexamined type of discrimination, which also can severely damage women financially, involves the purchase of goods and services.

The fact is that some vendors discriminate against women. There is growing evidence that sellers of certain products actually give men lower prices than women. In effect, they charge a gender tax. One such outrageous practice, discussed more fully in Chapter 5, was uncovered by the American Bar Foundation in 1990. The foundation studied hundreds of car dealerships in the Chicago area and discovered that, on average, women were charged a 40 percent higher profit markup than men. Emerging evidence suggests that price discrimination in other industries such as housing may cost a woman, over the course of a lifetime, many thousands of hard-earned dollars.

Divorce, caring for elderly parents, caring for children, outliving retirement funds, sexual discrimination—these are some of the reasons that make a woman's decision not to save and plan one of the riskiest gambles she will ever take. In fact, in view of the special financial risks women face over a lifetime, the decision not to plan really is no gamble at all—it's a sure-fire loser. The choice is not whether to save but how best to do it.

Planning helps. And though no amount of planning can guarantee we will always have enough savings to handle any of the special risks we face, failing to plan is an invitation for financial disaster.

Other Risks

We have identified certain special financial risks women face during our lives. What we have not explored are other perhaps even more important risks. These risks are certain general patterns and habits of thinking about money, which can crop up in almost every part of our lives and which, if uncorrected, can sabotage the best-laid financial plans. These habits of dealing with money often go unchallenged for years until some crisis forces us to look at the underlying ambiguities, conflicts, and misunderstandings. The next three chapters begin an exploration of three aspects of our relationship with money in our lives: (1) our relationship as borrowers or lenders in our families and friendships, (2) the role money plays in our marriages and relationships with men, and (3) the roles, myths, and conflicts that shape our view of money.

2. Those Who Borrow, Those Who Lend

> I don't like to lend my
> brother-in-law money.
> It gives him amnesia.
> —Henny Youngman

The cramped Western Union office in the corner of the supermarket on Lexington Avenue is little more than a box with a telephone. The surface of the desk in front of the clerk—who doubles at the checkout counter—is dominated by two kinds of slips, green for sending money, yellow for receiving money. The office opens at 9 AM and on one Saturday morning at ten after nine, the line is already seven anxious people deep.

As each one reaches the front of the line, questions are asked while forms are filled out. Those filling out the green forms ask:

"When will this get there?"

"Do they have to call your branch in Wichita or do you deliver?"

"How much does it cost to send $500?"

"Are you sure this'll get there before noon? It has to be before noon."

Those filling out yellow forms do not do the asking; they do the answering. They answer somewhat cryptic questions from the clerk:

"What's your sister's birthdate?"

"What is your mother's maiden name?"

"Who was Cousin Milliard's second wife?"

These are some of the secret questions posed by the Western Union clerk at the request of a Green Slip somewhere else to a Yellow Slip here at the Lexington branch. It's a password to have those Yellow Slips without identification prove they are who they say they are. The yellow and green slip transactions are part of the huge river of money flowing daily between family and friends.

Increasing numbers of Americans are providing financial support to persons living outside their households. According to a study by the United States Census Bureau, "Who's Helping Out?," over 6 million Americans contributed more than $18 billion annually (in 1985, the last year for which data is available) for such support, and 40 percent of this total represented contributions to the support of other adults, including ex-spouses and elderly parents. And women, the traditional caregivers, are being called on increasingly for this support. One reason is that American women are making more money than ever before. Moreover, as your income rises, so does the likelihood that you will be called on financially to support other adults. It is only human nature that those with less will try to get those with more to share the wealth or that we become more generous with family and friends as our income grows.

But are these transfers frictionless? And how does a person cope with being a family banker? The experience of the people you will meet in this chapter and my personal experiences suggest a strain not immediately apparent from a review of the numbers alone.

When You Can't Stop Giving Even Though the Giving Hurts

From outward appearances, Maura, a 34-year-old executive recruiter with three younger brothers, is the model of success. Originally from the Midwest, she graduated from Yale, lives in a fashionable neighborhood in Manhattan, and has an income from commissions in the six figures. But her voice rises an octave when she talks of the roller coaster that has been her financial life the past three years. "It never seems to end. Last year my mother's house burned down. There wasn't enough insurance to cover everything, and I basically had to carry Mom for months. If I hadn't, she would have been homeless."

Maura was happy to help her mother. She says she would do it again. But the crisis depleted her savings, and when her brother Patrick, a senior in college, called to ask for $2,000, she balked. The money was for a good cause— Patrick needed it to pay the remainder of his college bills— but Maura found she was becoming resentful of her role as family banker. That was not the reason she was putting in 70-hour weeks.

"I told him that when I was in college, Mom didn't have any money to send me. No one did. I had to make it on my own. He thinks I'm rich because I live on my own in New York. He doesn't stop to think that bills are bigger in New York. I'm just tired of cleaning everything up."

Maura's resentment about having to "clean everything up" reflects the enormous tension that can be a byproduct of the attempt to reconcile limited money resources with the needs of extended family and friends. The reaction I had to a letter from a relative three years ago mirrors the struggle Maura felt.

The morning after the letter arrived, I still hadn't opened it. My head ached from a night of restlessness. More than once I had accidentally-intentionally nudged my husband, hoping he would awaken to share my confusion; he didn't. She was blood of my blood, after all, family. I remember thinking, as I turned the letter over and over in my hands before opening it, that I already knew what it contained. The words would be different, the circumstances new, but the point would be the same: Send money now—or what, I wondered? "I'll be evicted." "My kids will go hungry." "The lights will be turned off."

How could I turn away from her basic need to survive, to keep her family together? But what about me? Would I ever be able to save for the children I wanted to have, for my own needs—just as real, if less urgent than hers. But what about the unspoken promises that bind you to your blood relatives? Hadn't we promised each other silently those many years ago always to fight the monsters of the dark together? My heroism fully summoned, I envisioned myself saving her, once again. I whimsically envisioned arresting the hand of the landlord before he threw them out on the street. But, fantasy fades after all, and looking down, I didn't see the magical spandex garb of Wonderwoman, but only an imitation silk dressing gown from Macy's. I opened the letter anyway, and I was not surprised to find that between a hurried "Dear" and a closing "Love always" was a compelling statement of financial need. I mailed the check that day, joining thousands of other Americans caught in the recurring conflict between money and love relationships.

Two core impulses are at war. One is to save yourself. The other is to save your loved one and also, perhaps, that vision of yourself as one who will sacrifice. A friend once told me of a special summer during her childhood. Her family had gathered at a lake house. A neighbor named John swam too far into the lake, developed a cramp, and was drowning. Her uncle immediately swam out into the lake to save the man. But John's survival instinct had made him panicky, and when the uncle tried to get an arm around John to pull them both to safety, John's arms tightened around the uncle's neck. Suddenly the uncle realized he was being pulled under. My friend sadly recalled that her uncle then had to decide to give up the rescue, use all his strength to break what he called "the deathgrip," and swim back to safety alone.

The decision whether to lend to a loved one doesn't always involve the choice of whether to drown yourself or break the "deathgrip." Sometimes, depending on the resources available, you can achieve the ideal solution of saving yourself and your loved one too. Sadly, though, sometimes the choice must be made. Because the decision often is at odds with an image you may have long held about yourself, an image that may in fact have become a part of you, making such a choice can put you in the soul's loneliest place—the space between conflicting images of yourself.

How to "Talk Money" to Those You Love

Perhaps there is no greater recipe for disaster than the mixture of money and love relationships. Money, whose language is calculation, cannot understand love, whose language tends to regard any "calculation" as "calculating" and, therefore, anathema to love. When love relationships become banking relationships, trouble is inevitable, unless a common language between borrowers and lenders can be found. We must find the emotional and financial vocabulary needed successfully to "talk money" to loved ones. To do this, we must begin to understand and correct some miscommunications between those who borrow and those who lend.

Loan requests, often awkward and painful for borrower and lender, rarely are made in straightforward language. The lender does not pick up the phone and hear, "Hello, Susan, this is your brother Mike. I need a $200 no-interest loan. I will repay you in ten days." Instead, Mike is likely first to talk about his kid's flu, his free-spending wife's latest outrage, Mom's troubles, and then, somewhere later in the conversation, mixed in with all these family ties, will be a money transaction. The language is indirect but often effective.

Sometimes the indirection is motivated by embarrassment and shame. Carolyn, a 42-year-old legal secretary and single parent who has borrowed often from her sister Joyce, will delay a loan request for weeks until she musters what she calls the "courage to be humiliated." "When I ask her for money," Carolyn explains, "it's like admitting to her we aren't equal anymore. I feel like I'm not measuring up in life."

Though Carolyn is a habitual borrower, she cares deeply about the effect of her loans on Joyce's budget. But the need is real, so the requests continue. And even those in our families who borrow less frequently can still feel deep shame for having to be a "burden." Elderly parents, for example, may refuse to ask for money even though, as inflation erodes the purchasing power of their fixed incomes, they are slowly sinking into poverty. Yes, the lending can hurt the lender's pockets. But the asking can hurt just as deeply.

One key to the development of a language enabling the clear communication about money to loved ones is to recognize that the language of love expresses a belief in absolutes, which defy measurement, while the language of money deals only in measurement. Love speaks of "forever," "infinity," and "pricelessness." For example, a relative whose loan request is denied may go away grumbling, "If you loved me, you'd help me out..." or some other similar platitude, such as "There are some things that can't be measured in dollars and cents." But money, whose historical development stemmed from the need to measure and thus to value commodities and services, only has meaning when applied to define "how much." Our capacity for love may be limitless, but our supply of money certainly is not. Therefore, loved ones who insist that you give commensurate with the amount of love on which the relationship is based are inviting you to do the conceptually impossible.

We thus arrive at the first axiom of family banking: Even though love has no measurement, money does. Because money's raison d'etre is measurement, those who use money without acknowledging that measurement is occurring are inviting confusion. You can no more deal in money without measurement than you can deal in water without wetness. And though Mike's sister Susan may deny to herself that an unpaid loan to family or friends is not measured like a "real loan," the measurement nonetheless occurs and the loan is repaid, if not from Mike, then by a subtraction of the dollars and cents available to Susan to meet her own needs.

Learning to Recognize Tribal Weapons

As we have seen, sometimes family members deal with internecine money issues in an indirect way, and the indirection is motivated by embarrassment and shame.

In other instances, however, the indirection is less innocuous, amounting to emotional blackmail. For example, Mary-Margaret, who is the first college graduate in her family, is often reminded by her siblings of the distance she has traveled from them, a reminder that is a condemnation of abandonment; her education is an abyss between them. Education can drive a properly conjugated verb right down the center of a family, dividing to one side those who say "them" from those who say "dem," those who say "isn't" from those who say "ain't," the "going to's" from the "gonna's," the "fixin to's" and the "gwonna's." To the siblings Mary-Margaret left behind, she is not progressing, she is abandoning. She is not soaring away, she is escaping.

What is at stake for Mary-Margaret and many other women in this situation is tribal loyalty. We are "family members" before we are schoolchildren, businesswomen, lawyers, teachers, nurses, wives, mothers, or anything else. Tribe members gather round us at birth and at death. The tribe is a part of our earliest identity. We feel, and come to depend on, the enveloping sense of tribe, of belonging, long before we learn to name it.

As we grow, daily signs assure us of our continuing membership in the tribe. The signs are subtle and powerful. Our heads are patted, we are smiled at, a warmth builds in the eyes of other tribe members when we enter the room. But as we explore worlds outside the family, we acquire foreign smells, smells other tribe members immediately can detect. Sniffing us over when we return to the tribe, our loving mother may say, "You've changed your hair." Tousling the new hair, she may work it with her fingers until it feels right to her again. She may notice—and take pride in or reject—a new habit of speech, a new assertiveness in cooking, a new awareness of the need to budget. Each new smell can be welcomed and become a part of the tribe or, as easily, it can be rejected. And rejection by the tribe can be painful. When Mary-Margaret turns down a family loan request, the tribe can respond with subtle, deeply hurtful weapons.

Many tribal weapons are not found in the words that are said but in the tone of what is said. Vowels can be amazingly malleable tools. Bend a vowel to the left and not the right, and what you get is a sneer rather than approval. You get hate rather than love. A lot of the vowels uncooperative family bankers hear curve severely to the left.

Breaking the Code of the Good Girl

These stories, which at first appear unconnected, form a pattern. The women behind the statistics who have become their families' bankers are the daughters, wives, and sisters who are the responsible ones, the pleasing ones, the "Good Girls." They are part of the answer to the Census Bureau's question, "Who's helping out?." And though the code of being a Good Girl varies from woman to woman, one rule a Good Girl never forgets is that she never abandons a crisis. If the ship is sinking and all others have fled, she hangs tough and can hear our entire society saying approvingly, "That's a Good Girl." If her elderly mother becomes too frail to care for herself and too poor to afford a nursing home, her brothers and sisters may occasionally send a small amount to help out, but it is the Good Girl who volunteers her already cramped home and stretched budget to take Mom in. If the marriage fails and the ex will not pay for child support, she gets a second or even a third job. People are apt to say of her, "She never thinks of herself." She believes it is always better to give than to receive, even if she cannot afford to give and even if the receiver never repays.

How to Resign as Family Banker

For those willing to pay the emotional price, a number of approaches may be useful for altering the financial expectations of family and friends. The first step common to each of these approaches is the characterization of the money to be transferred. Is it intended as a gift? As a loan? If the money is intended as a gift and you are the giver, you should already have decided you can forever forego the use of the money. Consider it gone. If you cannot afford the loss, you should reevaluate the characterization of the transfer and decide whether you should characterize the transfer as a long-term loan, rather than a gift. If the money is intended as a loan and you are the lender, you must treat the transfer as a bona fide loan and decide whether the prospective borrower meets your personal criteria to qualify for a loan.

Though the criteria you choose to use to evaluate prospective borrowers need not be the same as those of commercial banks, it is useful to have a working understanding of the standards used in the arms-length world of business and finance. Most banks use the following factors, applied with varied emphasis and priority, to decide whether or not to lend money:

1. Credit history of the borrower

2. Collateral available if the borrower defaults

3. Source of funds to repay

4. Net worth of borrower

The documentation that begins and ends the lending process would include, at a minimum, a loan application with prior credit references and a promissory note enforceable in a court of law if the borrower fails to repay.

Compared to the detailed procedures of commercial banks, the lending "procedures"—if a word so suggestive of a system can be used—of family bankers usually involve little or no documentation or criteria. At most, the only paper the family banker may have to document loan transactions totaling hundreds or even thousands of dollars is a canceled check bearing a confused description (or none at all) scribbled at the bottom such as "to Mike for kids."

The commercial bank differs from the family banker in attitude as well. The commercial banker feels justified in asking credit-screening questions and feels entitled to carry out the lending review process aggressively and with dispatch: a good applicant is approved, a bad applicant is rejected. By contrast, the family banker is likely to be the passive, overwhelmed target of an impassioned plea for help, and if the loan is made and not repaid on time, the family banker may find it is she, not the borrower, who feels guilty when the issue of repayment comes up. Many times, as a one-month loan ages into a two-month loan or even a one-year loan, it is the family banker who must tiptoe around the money issue, not the borrower, who may seem oblivious to the passage of time.

The family banker, when you stop to think about it, is one of the most remarkable lenders in the world. She charges no interest rate, assesses no late payment penalties, asks for no documentation, and, if the borrower fails to repay at all, the family banker even feels guilty and apologetic for bringing up the issue. Little wonder the family banker's teller window is visited so often.

For those of you comfortable asking your debtor to sign loan documents, the generic form of a promissory note in Table 2-1 should be helpful. Though the interest rate is omitted, you should avoid charging rates higher than local banks would charge because of the risk of violating your state's usury laws. After all, the idea is not to profit from these family loans but only to avoid losing money by increasing the likelihood of repayment.

Should you charge interest? Because of guilt, few family members feel comfortable charging interest. They feel heartless. Family members who charge interest feel as if they are acting too much like banks, even though ironically, that in effect is what they have become.

The other side of the issue is that some borrowers actually would prefer to be charged interest. They reason that if they pay interest, they need not feel like charity cases. To these borrowers, interest lessens the shame they feel in having to ask. Since it is better not to guess which feelings are at play in your family banking relationships, you should determine how you and your borrower feel about charging interest. You may be surprised to discover that the simple device of charging interest can relieve negative feelings on both sides, avoiding both resentment and shame.

PROMISSORY NOTE

In consideration of the receipt of _____ dollars (the "Debt") on the _____ day

of _____, I, _____ (name of borrower)

do hereby agree to repay said Debt at a per annum interest rate of _____ %[1] in equal

monthly installments of _____ dollars[2], payable in full by _____ (maturity date)

to _____ (your name)[3]

_____   _____

(name of borrower)   (date)

---

[1] You can choose not to charge interest.

[2] You can choose to make the Debt payable in one lump sum.

[3] Unlike typical promissory notes, this note has no clause making the borrower liable for the costs of collecting the note in case of a dispute. You can, if you wish, insert this type of provision.

TABLE 2-1

You also have to determine whether you are dealing with a habitual borrower who could find the funds from his or her own resources or whether you are dealing with a family member who has no other options, short term or long term.

The use of a promissory note could have a side benefit. Under certain circumstances, a taxpayer who has extended credit can deduct his or her losses if the borrower fails to repay. One condition to qualifying for this so-called "bad debt deduction" is that the taxpayer must have documents substantiating the existence of the loan. A promissory note or similar document would help you satisfy the substantiation requirement, making the loan appear less like a gift.

A less formal way of documenting the transfer is to send a letter to the borrower reflecting the amount of the transfer and expressly acknowledging the transfer as a loan. You should state somewhere in the letter language to the effect that, "I've decided to make you the loan you asked for and have enclosed a check for $X."

You should also indicate when you will need the money back. The form of transfer should always be a check, never cash, and you should take some care to ensure that the check adequately reflects that the transfer is a loan. Three steps should be taken. First, the description of the purpose of the check (in the bottom left hand corner of most drafts) should indicate that the transfer is a loan and note the repayment date and interest charged, if any. A simple, clear notation, such as "loan to Mike, repayment three months, no interest," should suffice. Second, you should write at the top of the check a notation indicating the date of the loan request and the full name of the person from whom you expect repayment, for example, "Reference: loan request March, 1989, from Mike Stomber." Third, you should retain a copy of the canceled check for your files.

In addition to possible tax benefits, another benefit of documenting a family loan is that the existence of documentation tends to firmly establish in the mind of the borrower that the transfer is a loan the lender expects to be repaid. The goal here is not to document the transaction in a way thorough enough to lay the foundation for a lawsuit against the borrower—though some family bankers may be comfortable taking this drastic step—but merely to acknowledge straightforwardly in writing what is occurring and therefore, hopefully, to decrease the chance of miscommunication and feelings of resentment or guilt.

But for most family bankers, the real problem is not so much establishing that the transfer is a loan but stopping the hemorrhages of their own budgets these family loans can cause.

An approach used successfully by some family bankers unable to deny a loan request altogether is a methodical scaling back of amounts lent. The success of the approach depends on the lender's ability to decrease the percentage of loans lent each time a loan request is made. Michelle, a 49-year-old bank vice president, handles transactions totaling hundreds of millions of dollars a year with admirable efficiency. Yet, when it came to dealing with family loan requests, Michelle felt inept. Michelle has a father who regularly borrowed $500 for one crisis or another. The unpredictability of the requests made it imposssible for Michelle and her husband to live within their budget. Her guilt and sense of daughterly obligation prevented her from denying the requests altogether even though she had her own problems with money—college tuition costs for her three children were eating away at the family's savings.

Finally, Michelle seized the initiative. She wrote a letter to her father explaining that she needed her earnings to support her children and the future dreams of her immediate family. She acknowledged the conflict the loan requests caused, affirmed her love for her father but—and this is the key—forced herself to send only $400, 80 percent of the amount requested, not the full $500. The effect on her father was that he slowly began to stop thinking of Michelle as the bank-of-first-resort for each crisis. His expectations lowered, he began to find other sources to make up the percentage of the loan request Michelle no longer filled. Over time, Michelle gradually has been able to lower the overall amounts of money her father borrows and, in fact, to reduce the frequency of his requests.

The effectiveness of the scaling back approach under-scores a fundamental trait of habitual borrowers: They will return to the bank as long as the bank keeps lending. They tend to be extraordinarily efficient and logical in their bor-rowing practices. If you demonstrate that you are willing to finance 100 percent of their needs, they logically approach you first and often. If you demonstrate you are willing to finance only 5 percent of their needs, they will approach you less often and probably only after being refused else-where.

What is lost when you refuse to lend? What is the awful consequence of not "coming through," of not being perfect, even once? For many, the real loss is the relinquishment of a role we have discussed before, the mantle of hero. For others, it is the loss of the vision of what our family ideally could be.

None of us is immune to the charm of the fantasy of an ideal, symbiotic family unit in which love, trust, food, and money all come with membership. These fantasies usually fall under the heading of "wouldn't it be nice if." For exam-ple, I am charmed by the concept of the "susu" among some Caribbean people. Susus are arrangements in which each member of a group of family or friends agrees to contribute a specified amount, say $100 each week or month, and each then takes turns at drawing out the whole bonanza.

Perhaps you have envisioned an idyllic arrangement in your own family. Perhaps you've envisioned an arrange-ment in which all members would contribute to a family fund, to be drawn against by those in need, no questions asked, so long as the fund was replenished within a rea-sonable period. But reality intervenes. And there will be those who will take money out but, when the time to repay the family fund arrives, either will not or will not be able to pay it back.

One critical observation: Family bankers who, after read-ing this chapter, believe they will be able to apply with instant success the communication tools and approaches discussed are in for a disappointment. There are no instant cures for a situation that usually has developed over many years. What we have embarked upon is a conscious re-examination and reshaping of family roles assumed over the course of a lifetime.

Self-inflicted emotional punishment obstructs our attempts to change our financial roles with family and friends. We suffer emotional pain as we attempt to bring quantification to roles and situations we traditionally have been taught are anathema to measurement. Family bankers who attempt to apply sensible banking criteria to family loan requests are apt to be greeted with scorn and indignation. Be prepared for shock, silence, anger.

But also be prepared to forgive the silence and the anger. After all, our goal is not to limit the sharing of concern or of love. The goal is not even to limit the sharing of money to one's spouse and children, relegating all other family and friends to the category of drains-on-assets. That is no remedy at all, except in the case of the most abusive money behavior. Rather, the goal is to assess realistically how much and under what circumstances giving is helpful both to the giver and to the receiver. Sometimes saying no will mean disaster, but other times, perhaps many more times, it will begin the slow process towards financial health and independence for both lender and borrower.

Perhaps no greater test of adulthood exists than the challenge to decide which roles we will play and which we will discard or modify. Even to say that we *decide* these roles is to overstate the volition involved. The roles, such as those of family banker or borrower, are acquired not so much through force of will or exercise of discretion as through inadvertence and habit of inertia. We lack a plan of action or even the time to prepare a plan. The momentum of unforeseen emergencies and crises seems too compelling to afford us the luxury of examining the wisdom of actions and carries us along for years, producing a financial status whose origins we do not recognize, prompting us to wonder how we got ourselves into this fix in the first place. The trouble is, we did not get ourselves into this fix. We failed to keep ourselves out of it.

3. His Money, Her Money

"No whale, no cause, is greater than our love," Sean Penn is reported to have declared when he and Madonna were an item. At a loss to express the perfect bliss of being in love, we try words soaring way up above, high, higher, beyond the clouds, above the affairs of mundane, everyday life. Everlasting, blissful, mythical, majestic, ineffably joyful love—that's what many of us, like Sean, believe marriage should be. The vision of the ideal marriage rarely is expressed in terms at or below sea level.

This matter of money, however—it's a sea level thing. Its management is closer to the kind of practical sorting out that occurs after, well, love-making, when we reclaim limbs and lips from the amorphous, unified jumble. When we get down to the business of being separate again, as when we sort out paying bills, we sometimes run into difficulty. Most of that difficulty, it seems, stems from an undefined feeling that the kind of love and marriage we ought to have is the supernal, way-up-in-the-sky kind, while the kind of marriage where money is (hold your nose) *managed*, is the sea level kind. We sometimes daydream that, "If we just had enough money, we'd be able to spend every waking moment together, just staring into each other's eyes, eating mangoes, walking along the beach." Or maybe we think we would be like the independently wealthy married characters played by Robert Wagner and Stephanie Powers in the T.V. series "Hart to Hart," free on a whim to leave household affairs to our trusty man-servant and chase intriguing mysteries all over the globe. Ah, surely, love would blossom eternal. But the fact of the matter is that even for couples who do not really have to worry about money, money fights occur (witness the publicized acrimonious divorces of the real-life superrich) and learning as a couple to come to grips with money needn't dim love's light one milliwatt. It may, in fact, help to keep your marriage from becoming one of the 50 percent of all marriages that, like Sean's and Madonna's, fail. So, let's start the sorting out.

Money and Marriage Go Together Like a Horse and Carriage?

Studies show that women in married couples do better financially than women heading households alone. As one report observed, "Women who are married are four times more likely as those heading families alone to have a family income of $30,000 or more." This fact is not all that surprising when you consider that married women are more likely than single heads of households to draw from the resources of two incomes. So, as a general statement, it appears that marriage brings identifiable and significant financial benefits to women.

But studies also show that men and women fight more about money than about any other topic. Part of the reason, it seems, is that women are acquiring more economic resources within the marriage. Between 1967 and 1981, for example, the number of marriages increased by 6.4 million, but the number of married households in which the husband was the sole-earner fell by 5.3 million. By 1981, 5.9 million wives earned more than their husbands. This figure represented over 12 percent of all married couples, and the trend has grown more and more pronounced since then. Heightened by the emergence of women as capable breadwinners, the battle over money rages across the dinner table and in the bedroom, appearing at some period and in some guise in almost all marriages. Sometimes the battle is a subtle shifting of roles and expectations: Who should pay the taxes, who should control the checkbook? For most couples, the money issue emerges first during dating—who should pay or appear to pay the check at dinner—and, if not addressed, it can begin a slow, silent erosion of the relationship. Many couples sweep the issue of how they relate to money under the rug, postponing it for consideration after they have tackled what they view as more pressing issues. But, sooner or later, certainly after marriage, the rug gets rather lumpy, and those pesky unanswered money issues can resurface, only this time in fights and hurt feelings that seem to build over nothing.

One of the best ways to avoid problems with money issues is to address them head-on and early. How do you know when you and your mate are headed for money trouble? One of the surest signs is a hesitancy to talk straightforwardly about money. Because it is almost certain that money will come up as a challenge at some point in a serious relationship, your inability to put it on the table for discussion means you probably will lack the basic communication skills to address problems that may arise. Another telltale sign of future trouble is feelings of resentment about the linkage in your relationship between money and power. For in personal relationships, as cynical as it may sound, money and power almost always are aligned. This does not mean all the power in the relationship is aligned with the partner having the most money, but it does mean that if your relationship is typical, the mate who earns substantially more than the other also is far more likely to control lots of key decisions in the relationship, decisions ranging from which house to purchase to who will give up his or her job to relocate to who will stay home with a child who gets sick. Money may even determine whether one of you has an affair. As author Lewis Lapham noted (with perhaps tongue in cheek) in his book *Money and Class in America*, "The incidence of marital infidelity rises in conjunction with an increase in income. Of the married men earning $20,000 a year, only 31 percent conduct extracurricular love affairs; of the men earning more than $60,000, 70 percent."

To begin to identify whether you and your mate are relating poorly about money, answer the following questions:

1. Do you ever feel embarrassed if you have to pay for items while in public with your mate?

2. Does your mate ever feel embarrassed if you have to pay for items while he is in public with you?

3. Do you feel a need to keep up appearances by hiding your mate's inability to earn more or his inability to handle finances in any way, such as budgeting or paying for taxes?

4. Do you resent (a) consulting your mate about how to spend money you earn or (b) your mate's failure to consult you about how he spends money he earns?

If you have answered any of these questions with a "yes," then, chances are, you feel uncomfortable about the way power and money are aligned in your relationship; you or your mate are putting effort, perhaps significant effort, into masking your money status or financial abilities. Where does the discomfort begin? As it turns out, the trouble can start early.

What You Learned from Mom and Dad

Most of us are born as the newest arrivals to a financial battle already in its full throes. "The first recollection I have of money, that it was going to be important, or it was a problem, was one night hearing my parents argue after they thought we were asleep," recalls Marsha. "I couldn't make out all the words, I couldn't tell what it was, but my father sounded drunk. He was accusing my mother of spending money on something. I cracked my door to listen. She was crying." Marsha couldn't tell what "it" was, but from then on, she knew money was important. It was so important, it could come between mother and father, and it was whispered about at night. It was, and is, the age-old struggle to make ends meet.

And even if yours was a family in which money was never talked about openly or in which money was never an issue of crisis, all of us learn our early lessons about how men and women relate as a couple to money by watching how our folks do it. This is true whether you were raised in a two-parent household or, as is increasingly the case, by a single parent. What we see as young audiences to fights or negotiations, disharmony or harmony teaches us volumes of lessons. We learn lessons, for example, about the desirability or undesirability of going it alone or lessons about how much money a woman should control in a marriage to avoid conflict.

What did you learn as an early audience? For one, studies show that men are taught, and in turn teach, that boys should outearn girls. One of daddy's chief roles, if he is to be respected by you and your playmates, is to work. If daddy lies around on the sofa all day, something is wrong. In my first year of college, my dorm monitor was the daughter of an independently wealthy man who seemed to her and her childhood friends to "loaf" around the house all day while the other non-embarrassing dads went off to catch the train. As she put it to me, "I just didn't understand why Arthur didn't work." This image of what men should do or earn, and what women should handle or not handle, persists today. And even though the type of family structure that would have made such an arrangement possible is no longer the norm—after all, two-parent households account for only about 25 percent of all households today—the shadow dream of a nuclear family, such as those in "Father Knows Best" or "Ozzie and Harriet" or "The Donna Reed Show," awakens startlingly vivid and powerful tugs. To an important degree, we still are controlled by these pre-1960s images, and they surface today in mild and severe conflicts between men and women over money's role in the home. As reported in *The Journal of Marriage and the Family*, a study of professional women, including those who view themselves as the intellectual equals of their husbands, showed that women nonetheless continue to consider childcare and housework as their responsibilities as wives.

Returning for a moment to Donna Reed's house, what we see is that men are expected to prove their worth in life through, among other ways, demonstrating financial prowess. "The critical difference in the socialization of men and women is that, despite recent advances, women are socialized primarily to occupy a family role.... Men, on the other hand, learn both economic and family roles," according to sociologist Carolyn Dexter. Little girls are taught in countless ways, both subtle and overt, that there is something unwomanly or unfeminine about having too much to do with money. Numbers are for boys; counting is for boys. Some studies even show that schoolteachers subconsciously steer little girls away from mathematics. And the woman who concerns herself too much in the affairs of money runs the risk of being placed somewhere along a rather unsavory continuum: she can be anything from a gold digger to that ultimate exchanger of emotions for cash, the prostitute. In this regard, it is intriguing that prostitutes indeed are referred to as "pros," meaning practitioners of "the world's oldest profession," while the word "professional" used in almost any other context would mean a person capable of earning a living through a respected career pursuit.

The Ghost of Donna Reed

Into the marriage march the ghost images of Donna Reed and the lot, all jostling and elbowing for a place among the financial realities of making ends meet. Men and women who consider their marriage "traditional"—meaning he's the breadwinner and she's the keeper of hearth and home—can be caught repeatedly in spots where image and reality do not mesh. It's hard to squeeze Donna Reed into a two-income reality. Yes, she may think it would be nice if she could stay home with the kids while he works, but the lifestyle that in 1950 could be supported by one salary now takes two. So off she goes to work, and in comes money created by her independent labors. But along with the money, attached to each dollar, comes a new desire for recognition of her ability to do what once was (and perhaps on some level still is) considered solely a manly thing. With the wife's increased financial independence, she also acquires a greater voice in making decisions that previously may have been her husband's sole domain. As sociologist Veronica Nieura has observed, "The independent financial base provided by employment provides women with an increased sense of competence, gives women more power within the marriage, and increases their influence in decision-making." Donna Reed is in voice.

Conflict is almost inevitable. A famous television commercial for a perfume suggested that women can reconcile the conflict if they (to paraphrase) "bring home the bacon, fry it up in a pan, but never, never, never let him forget he's a man; cause you're a woman." This feat, even wrapped in the ambience of Madison Avenue's Superwoman fantasy, seems pretty impossible.

Sorting Out Money Issues Between You and Him

Let's assume you and your mate are willing to try to establish lines of communication about money. First, choose a time to talk solely about money. Clear an hour or two of time unfettered by television, kids, work, or friends. Second, make a promise to yourself and get his agreement to talk regularly, no matter what the outcome of the first discussion. Now, let's begin.

Ideally, your discussion should center first around the money issues on which you agree. In that way, you set a positive tone for the discussion. This cushion of goodwill will be a helpful emotional pillow to fall back on when the conversation gets more heated. Then, take a pad and draw a line down the middle. Label the left hand side "Five Bad Money Habits I Have That You'd Like to Change" and the right hand side "Five Bad Money Habits You Have That I'd Like to Change." Before you begin to list items, make a commitment to work on changing one habit per month. Don't try to change more rapidly. You'll find changing one habit each month hard enough. Now, list the first item on the left hand side. This will be a habit he'd like to change in you. Why begin with you? Well, the fact is that if you've taken the trouble to go out and buy a book to help you understand yourself better financially, you are probably more comfortable than he in opening yourself up for exploration. Also, if you show your spouse you are willing to take a dose of criticism from him first, he is less likely to feel threatened when it is your turn to swing. After the first item is listed on the left hand side, ask your spouse, "How much does this habit bother you?" Also, try to find out when he notices the behavior—is it only when money is scarce, is it only noticed around tax time, only when other sensitive issues come up, such as your family or your sexual independence? Then, go on to the second item on the left hand side, repeating the procedure of talking about the item before you proceed to item three, and so on until you have covered all five items on the left hand side. While you are going over items on your side, resist the urge to begin to discuss his habits. If you do this, the discussion is less likely to degenerate into a point-counterpoint or worse.

After you've completed your side, and if you still have at least half an hour of quiet time left, start on the right side of the sheet. If you have less than that left, schedule another hour to talk about his habits. In the meantime, you and he will have time to digest what behavioral changes must occur to diminish or eliminate the issues on the left side of the pad.

The War of Independence

The above exercise will help you identify certain differences in how you and your spouse deal with money, such as who is the spender and who is the hoarder. But beyond these sometimes superficial differences, other kinds of issues likely to emerge from this type of exercise will center around *independence*. For the amount of money you control in a relationship will in large part determine your independence. The stories are legion about women who stay in marriages because they either cannot or believe they cannot survive financially without their mates. This is true for women who are affluent as well as for those who are merely keeping their head above water.

For example, my hairdresser, Katina, is a 26-year-old with the wisdom of a 90-year-old. Katina is from Tobago, the tiny tropical island just north of Venezuela. She is six months pregnant, and as she moves around the chair doing my hair, her belly occasionally bumps me. Her mother died when Katina was only eleven. Katina remembers what her mother endured for family and money:

"My father only cared for himself. He beat her up so much. We, he didn't abuse though. My mother, though, he had to own 24-7, all the time.

"She was beautiful and 20 years too young for him. He was a controllin' man with his money. He beat her so many time because his money couldn't control her though. I couldn't recognize her, my own mother, sometime, after the beating. She was just a monster in my mother's clothes.

"Me, I don't take that off a man. She, though, she said she had no way else to feed us, six kids you know."

Katina has done pretty well for herself. She and her husband own a two-family house in Brooklyn, living in one part and renting the other for $800 a month. This is a woman who counts her pennies. For those who do not, she has but one contemptuously uttered word: "fools." She is a long way from Tobago and a long time from those bad days, but it is clear from listening to her that the image of that "monster in her mother's clothes" continues to drive her determination to become financially independent.

The same perception of financial dependence that controlled Katina's mother keeps a woman I know married to an investment banker earning nearly $1 million a year, tied to a marriage devoid of fidelity. Is she really financially dependent? Probably not. But she believes she is, so she is. One author tells the story of how circus elephants are trained not to run away. When an elephant is first captured in the wild, its leg is tethered to the ground by a thick metal chain driven deep into the ground by an iron stake. The elephant nonetheless struggles to break the chain, sometimes so hard that it bloodies its leg in the attempt to escape. But, soon, the elephant learns that struggle as it may, that chain won't break, and its will to fight dwindles. Its struggling ceases. Eventually, the trainer is able to replace the metal chain with a lighter tether, and even the largest elephant can be controlled by just a thin rope.

Perceptions of dependence can be just as strong a chain, and be just as disabling, as true dependencies. Women who perceive that they cannot behave in certain ways in their marriages or relationships lest they upset the alignment of financial power are effectively tethered, whether that tether is the inability to choose what city the couple ultimately settles in or whose parents the kids spend summers with or who decides how to spend spare cash. They are modifying their behavior in response to power, whether perceived or real, whether made of iron or gossamer.

Heading Off Trouble: Antenuptial Agreements

Some couples try to head off trouble before marriage (or before they become "significant others") by entering into antenuptial agreements. Antenuptial agreements are designed to resolve contractually prickly issues, such as division of property acquired before or during marriage, and are enforceable in most states if drafted correctly. Antenuptial agreements can be immensely valuable if the marriage ends in divorce by helping a couple avoid costly, contentious court battles, which often enrich the lawyers on both sides while whittling away the dispersable estate. However, to ensure that the antenuptial agreement is drafted correctly, you should consult a lawyer. Another reason to have lawyers involved on both sides during the drafting of the agreement is that it diminishes the chance that one of the spouses will be able to have the agreement voided by arguing that he or she did not fully know what he or she was doing when the agreement was signed. For all their value, however, antenuptial agreements, in the view of many couples, are repugnant to the very notion of marriage: They view it as a pre-planned divorce.

Whether it is to your advantage to enter an antenuptial agreement also depends on whether your marital estate will be adjudicated in a state with community property laws. Community property laws, as a general matter, divide all property earned or acquired during the marriage as the joint property of both husband and wife. The result is that upon divorce, the bulk of the estate is divided fifty-fifty. Property owned by either spouse prior to marriage generally is considered non-community or "separate" property and is not subject to the fifty-fifty division. Currently, there are seven community property states: Arizona, California, Idaho, Louisiana, New Mexico, Washington, and Texas.

Divorce

When the once unthinkable becomes the inevitable, and you and your spouse begin considering divorce, your entire financial picture should be re-examined. For, as we discussed in Chapter One, women are much more likely than men to suffer deep and prolonged financial hardship from divorce.

Besides dealing with the emotional issues of failure and the loss of the dream of a life's mate, the woman living through the nightmare of divorce may also find herself sitting bolt upright in the middle of the night worrying about money.

Whether your divorce leaves you strapped will depend a lot on the cooperation of your ex-spouse. If the divorce is amicable, if both parties genuinely strive to take away from the marriage only what they fairly earned, and if both can be reasonable about child custody, the divorce can go quickly and smoothly. But you cannot count on this happening. Your divorce could be nasty. Few situations so inflame the human imagination for cruelty than the prospect of an impending divorce. Once-loving spouses have resorted to wiping out joint accounts, selling homes without the other's consent, kidnapping children, disrupting the other's workplace, destroying property (cars are often the target), assault, and yes, even murder. Make no mistake about it: You need to prepare for divorce more seriously than you have prepared for anything before in your life.

Dividing Property: Playing Smart in the Allocation Game

Though dividing property upon divorce can be messy legally and nasty emotionally, it really involves only two basic steps: asset identification and asset allocation.

One of the first serious mistakes many women make is in failing to identify all marital assets. Most of us can identify large visible assets, such as the house, the cars, the furniture. Often overlooked, however, are intangible assets or contract rights, assets potentially far more valuable than the ones before your eyes. These overlooked assets include

Insurance policies

Social Security benefits

Pension plan and other retirement benefits

Professional degrees or other tools of the trade

Tax exemptions for children

As an ex-spouse, you may be entitled to Social Security benefits based on your husband's average lifetime earnings provided that your marriage lasted at least ten years. The rules governing these benefits can be difficult to follow, but basically you are entitled to benefits in two situations. One, if you are unmarried, at least 62 years old, and your ex-spouse collects Social Security, you are entitled to benefits. Two, even if he is not actually collecting benefits, you are entitled to receive them if you are at least 62 and have been divorced for two years or more. How much you get depends, among other things, on how much he earned. To find out, order Form SSA-7004 from the local Social Security Administration office. Through this form, you will be able to find out your spouse's (or your) lifetime FICA earnings. And, remember, even though you may be entitled to benefits as a divorced spouse, the Social Security Administration will not act until you apply for benefits. Do not expect a check to show up in the mail automatically.

A divorced spouse meeting the qualifications above is entitled to an amount equal to 50 percent of the monthly amount her ex-husband is entitled to receive, whether or not he has applied for benefits. For example, if your husband, Jack, is entitled to receive $700, you would be entitled to receive $350. Your entitlement does not decrease Jack's, however. He still gets his full $700. Moreover, Jack's current spouse also gets an entitlement, irrespective of whether you also get benefits. There is one catch, though. The amount any spouse or ex-spouse receives is limited to the greater of

1. What you'd get based on your individual life earnings or

2. What you'd get as a spouse or ex-spouse based on Jack's life earnings

To return to our example, suppose that based on your individual lifetime earnings, you would be entitled to receive $300 per month. As Jack's ex-spouse, you'd be entitled to receive $350. Does this mean your total benefit would be $650? No such luck. Your total benefit would be $350. As you can see, for women who outearn their spouses, there really is no extra Social Security spousal benefit. But if you do not outearn your spouse, it will pay to apply for spousal benefits even after divorce.

As for private pensions, the value of these can be divided by a court using a "qualified domestic relations order." Through this order, you may be able to obtain your share of your husband's pension (or he may be able to obtain his share of your pension) in a lump sum or in installments over the course of your retirement years.

Insurance policies are also a large and sometimes overlooked asset. As we discuss further in Chapter 12, you could become the "co-owner" of your husband's life insurance policy. As co-owner, you would retain the right to designate beneficiaries and transfer the policy, despite divorce. But, if you did not take this step, your best tack is to negotiate for the right to continue to be carried as a beneficiary on your husband's policy, even if he is remarried. If you expressly retain this right in the divorce decree and settlement, it will be more difficult for the next wife to shut you out of the life insurance proceeds. You also may wish at this time to consider taking out a policy on your husband's life in case he dies before he finishes paying alimony.

Professional degrees and achievements earned or accomplished during marriage also are major assets you should not overlook. Did he graduate from law, medical or dental school, complete accounting courses, become vice president? Identifying these degrees or achievements is important because, unless they are on the table at the asset identification state, they will not be available for the asset allocation stage.

Another asset many divorcing women fail to identify as a bargaining chip are exemptions for children. Federal tax law entitles the custodial parent to exemptions for children in his or her care. However, the custodial parent (usually the wife) can choose to give away some or all of these exemptions to improve her bargaining position with respect to other assets.

After you and your spouse have put all assets on the table, the next step is to assign them value and to allocate how much of that value goes into your column and how much goes into his.

Certain assets are fairly simple to value. Your house, for example, can be assigned a market value, depending on the prices of similar houses recently sold in the area. Life insurance policy benefits also can be easily ascertained. However, determining the value of other assets, especially intangible ones such as a professional degree, can be troublesome and the source of much negotiation. Your spouse's or your degree, for example, can be assigned value in a number of ways, none entirely satisfactory because of the inherent difficulty of determining just how much a degree, as opposed to, say dedication at work, contributed to his or your earnings. As a starting point, do not let your lawyer bargain for less than the maximum salary earned during any one year of marriage multiplied by the number of years you think you should receive financial assistance. The goal here is not always alimony—you may have out-earned him, in which case you could end up paying him alimony—but to maximize your identified contribution. If he ends up paying alimony, the larger your identified contribution to the attainment of his degree, the greater your bargaining power to increase alimony payments. Or, if you end up paying alimony, your identified contribution to his degree may be used as a bargaining chip to subtract from the amount of alimony you would otherwise have to pay.

Speaking of alimony, do not count on it. Surveys and studies indicate that only 20 percent of divorced women receive any alimony. Some financial analysts put the figure even lower. Deena Katz, a financial planner from Miami, estimates that only 17 percent of divorced women receive alimony. Part of the reason women are receiving so little is the growing trend in states to deny the grant of alimony except in those cases involving a "lengthy" marriage and where financial need is demonstrated. What constitutes a "lengthy" marriage? It varies from state to state. California, for example, generally views as "lengthy" any marriage longer than ten years. Other states have even tougher standards. According to Ms. Katz, in Illinois, "Unless you've been married for 30 years, forget it." And do not forget, when you calculate the value of alimony payments, that, unlike child support, alimony is fully taxable to the recipient and deductible to the payer. So, the alimony payments you receive will be reduced by the tax bite.

You should have all your marriage property agreements (antenuptial, divorce) drafted by an attorney. Keep in mind, though, as you select an attorney, that not all domestic relations lawyers are equally capable. And you must be especially conscientious to make sure that you select quality representation. To interview a lawyer to handle the drafting of an antenuptial agreement or any other issue dealing with spousal property division, you should have several questions in hand. One question you should ask is whether he or she is accustomed to representing plaintiffs or defendants in these matters—it makes a difference. Over years of practice, lawyers tend to acquire habits of mind and skills more suited to the representation of one side or another. Lawyers who usually represent the spouse seeking property from the other spouse become accustomed to aggressive, offensive-minded motions or negotiation strategies needed to bring plaintiffs a good result. Lawyers accustomed to defending against such thrusts, though no less aggressive, acquire a different kind of skill. The point here is that you hire a lawyer because of the tactical advantage he or she can give you, and a lawyer accustomed to representing interests aligned with yours is more likely to know helpful ins and outs. Another question you should pose is what kind of strategies the lawyer would use to counter a retaliatory bankruptcy filing. Over recent years, spouses, overwhelmingly husbands, have come up with a rather inventive use of the bankruptcy laws to circumvent divorce settlements. Wife wins a favorable divorce settlement giving her, for example, the right to half the proceeds of a sale of the house. As part of the divorce settlement, the judge orders a lien placed on the house to protect wife's interests. However, shortly after the divorce decree is entered, husband retaliates by filing for bankruptcy. The effect of the bankruptcy filing is to remove the lien in those states which protect certain of the debtor's assets, such as a house, from liens. Appellate courts have split over whether to allow bankruptcy protections to be used to circumvent a divorce decree, and the United States Supreme Court (in the case of *Farrey v. Sanderfoot*), is expected to put the issue to rest soon. This is the type of issue about which your domestic relations lawyer should be familiar, and a well-posed question from you can certainly ferret out the weak from the capable.

You should also have all major financial documents— wills, insurance policies, pension plan documents, tax returns, deeds and so on—collected in one place, where you and your lawyer can readily find them. And make copies. Try to gather them up as soon as you feel divorce looming. It will be much harder to get them from an unco-operative spouse once the nastiness begins in earnest.

Reclaiming your financial separateness through divorce is not about punishment. "Winning is not necessarily the best settlement," notes Cicily Carson Maton of Aequus of Chicago, a company specializing in financial planning for divorce. "Winning is getting you ready for the rest of your life."

To get to the rest of your life, you'll need both financial and emotional resources. Don't try to do it all alone. Where you can find strength from family and friends or hired experts, use it. One useful reference is Judith Blithe's *Dollars and Sense of Divorce.* Beyond the advice you can garner from books and articles, consider hiring expertise in financial planning, and always hire an attorney. Identify what an expert does best, then use her or him only for that purpose. You should not, for example, use your lawyer as a substitute shoulder to cry on, especially if that shoulder costs you $300 an hour. On the other hand, some sources such as Aequus of Chicago may be able either to help you identify and assemble the financial and legal expertise you will need or give you good referrals. They can help you pull together the other professionals you will need. Or, you can act as your own coordinator and assemble a competent team consisting of a lawyer, perhaps a psychologist or psy-chiatrist, and a financial adviser. While you may believe you cannot afford this kind of help, if you have even a moderate amount of assets, you probably cannot afford not to have such a team.

A Woman of Independent Means

For the most part, to have independence, you must also be a woman of independent means. As noted, money and power are more or less aligned. True, some women whose spouses outearn them nonetheless control the consuming power or the budgeting power in the marriage. But most women who have few or no resources of their own feel almost powerless to sway important decisions in the house-hold or, for that matter, in their lives. And in light of the possibility (some would say probability) that the marriage may one day fail, it is incumbent on most of us to plan seriously for financial self-sufficiency, whether or not married. The biggest struggle for many of us is to overcome the sense that in planning for self-sufficiency, we somehow are straddling, planting one foot inside the marriage on the sacred ground of hope and the other, disloyal foot in the divorce court.

Here are some rules of thumb that can be helpful. One, maintain a credit history independent of your husband's. If you need a credit card, it should be obtained in your own name. You should also monitor the card's use. Don't fall into the trap of allowing a spouse to run up charges you cannot cover. The issue of joint or separate credit may seem trivial, but when it becomes a problem, it is usually gigantic.

Two, make sure that when you co-sign or guarantee loans, you receive an identifiable financial benefit and that you at least share control over the source of income used for repayment. For example, women married to men owning small businesses or having professional practices sometimes are asked by their spouses to co-make or guarantee business loans. These loans can run into the hundreds of thousands of dollars or more. Trusting their spouses to operate these businesses, some women have no input into decisions affecting the company or practice. Of course, as long as the business is bringing in enough money and the economy is buoyant, operational problems can be masked. But if the business fails, and you have signed on as a co-maker or guarantor of these loans, you're stuck. A good rule of thumb is don't put your money where your brain is not welcome. Don't incur personal liability for enterprises over which you have no decisional or operational control or which you just don't understand.

Three, maintain at least one separate bank account even if you also maintain joint accounts with your spouse. One of the first bright ideas a separating spouse gets is to wipe out all joint accounts. That may leave you without any cash for monthly living expenses. Remember the "mad money" your mom or dad made you pin to your blouse or tuck in your jeans before you went on a date? It was always enough money to get you back home. Well, in a sense, women should keep at least six month's living expenses, mad money, in a separate account for just those times when, to our amazement and against all expectations, life goes mad.

Four, plan your pension to account for the possibility of divorce or widowhood. Some women depend almost exclusively on their husband's job pension for almost all of their retirement fund. But is a divorced wife entitled to pension benefits of her ex-husband? Maybe. As a general matter pension funds are payable only to the employee or, upon his or her death, to the beneficiary as designated by the deceased spouse. Upon divorce, your interest in your spouse's pension may terminate if he changes the beneficiary designation, an action he is likely to take. Some courts have taken the view that a wife's contribution to her husband's ability to earn makes pension benefits earned during a marriage a part of the marriage estate, divisible upon divorce. As we have discussed, you may be able to persuade a court to divide the value of pension funds and accumulations using a qualified domestic relations order. But not all jurisdictions are friendly. And not all judges are agreeable. Do not count on the court ruling in your favor. Many of these decisions are a matter of balancing equities—fairness—and what is fair in one case may not be considered fair in another.

Five, prepare, and get your spouse to prepare, a will. One traditional marriage ceremony anticipates widowhood: You are bound "till death do you part." But most people feel uncomfortable preparing wills because it necessarily involves contemplating mortality. Who can really blame them? Nonetheless, you and your spouse really have only two choices: Either you two will decide how your hard-earned assets will be divided or the state will do it for you. When a resident of a state dies intestate (without a will), the state's intestacy laws take over, cranking out who gets how much. How much a wife gets under these intestacy laws depends in many cases on whether there are surviving children. Depending on the state, as the surviving spouse, you may get it all, half, one-third, or some other share. Most states will not leave 100 percent to the surviving spouse if there are children. So, if you and your husband intend to leave 100 percent of the property to each other, you must expressly state your desires in a properly-executed will.

Creating a mad money account, funding a pension plan, or taking some of the other recommended precautions is a lot easier when you have learned sound strategies for saving and budgeting. Part II explores several strategies that should help to get you well on your way to becoming a woman of at least some independent means.

4. Roles, Myths, Conflicts

What Money Stands for in Your Life

The story of money in our lives is rife with symbolism. Money often "stands for" something else. Money can stand as a symbol of competence. If two engineers of equal age work in the same industry and one makes $75,000 per year and the other makes $25,000, most people make the unspoken assumption that the first engineer is more competent than the second. Or, if a parent raises two children, one who moves out of the house and supports herself independently and the other who remains at home, friends and relatives—and even the parents—may assume the adult who remains at home is less competent at what he or she does.

Money can stand as a symbol of power. The parent who, having lost an argument, insists on winning anyway "as long as you are under my roof" is using this power. The unspoken bargain the losing side is reminded of is that since the parent owns the roof, the loser must obey seemingly unrelated rules concerning haircuts, TV viewing habits, and so on. The husband or wife who sets the house rules on which items are "necessities" and which are "luxuries" because he or she is the higher earner is also using money as power.

Money can stand for intelligence and strength and lead to mimicry. For example, with the emerging economic dominance of the Japanese and Germans have come increasing signs of cultural mimicry. American businesspeople, convinced that all things Japanese are "better," are soul-searching to determine how they might better adopt Japanese business practices. Putting aside serious doubts that Japanese business practices can be wholesale transplanted to a society as diverse and independent as America's, an interesting corollary phenomenon is emerging. Now, businesspeople who "think like Japanese" are sought after, and a businessperson trying to intimidate office rivals may hang Japanese art in the office, take vacations to the Orient, sprinkle conversation with Japanese phrases, and so on. In effect, while the 1960s up-and-coming office intimidator may have mimicked the cowboy macho of John Wayne, today's intimidator is more and more likely to mimic samurai warriors.

Money can stand as a symbol of love. It is often used as a substitute for expressions of love or expressions of fear of losing love. Mary, who lends money to her friend Susan, may feel she needs to give away money, lest she herself be given away emotionally. Deep down she may believe Susan is far more interesting, valuable, alive than she, and to make up for her perceived deficiencies, she brings money to the friendship. Or, a parent who finds it difficult to say, "I love you," may instead bring gifts or stuff an extra bill in her child's jeans. Or, a woman may shower her boyfriend with expensive watches, clothes, and money, unaware that she is acting out of fear of losing him. Faced with his infidelity, she may in angry confusion yell, "But why? I gave you everything!" Or even more tellingly, "At least tell me why you did it—you owe me that much for all I've done for you." Here, money may have been used as a talisman, to ward off evidence of telltale disloyalty that she was unable or unwilling to address until it was unavoidably in front of her eyes.

The story of money in our lives is rife with myth. In our roles as wife, daughter, girlfriend, worker, or mother, we also assume money roles. Many of these roles are our everyday attempts to live up or down to a "myth." The genesis of the family role is sometimes hard to pinpoint, but once it starts, it is difficult to shake off. Having been designated as the strongest, brightest, kindest, or whatever, we learn to act the role, and it becomes us. For example, we may find ourselves resentful but unable to change our pattern of "coming to the rescue," even if the rescue hurts us more than it helps those we think we are rescuing.

The Hero Woman

One of the most adhesive roles to discard, for those who wish to peel it off, is that of the "hero." Hero qualities are so adhesive because their existence seems to spring not only from the family member playing the hero but also from other family members. The hero seems to acquire an identity onto which many qualities other than the initial strength can be projected. Thus, the family member who has become a hero because she is nurturing may also come to be expected to "lead" the family financially or even spiritually. In fact, the whole idea of a hero becomes an almost spiritual role, with family heroes serving as minor deities or, perhaps more accurately, little saints.

Because so many general aspects of leadership can be projected onto their identities, family heroes can be sucked into vacuums created by other family members' inertia. Rather than doing what is obviously necessary, family members may instead merely watch a problem grow, waiting for the hero to "do something." This inertia can be disastrous when the problem is personal finance. For by the time the family hero arrives at the scene, the amount of money needed to rescue the situation can be enlarged grotesquely by interest and late penalties.

To peel off the role of hero, or any other for that matter, can be painful. But the first step is one taken here—recognition.

Looking inside for clues to recognizing whether money's position in our lives is imbalanced is a tricky search. The relationship can be so riddled with conflict and contradiction. And, too, much of the conflict seeps in from cultural messages.

Women as Property: "Who Giveth This Bride?"

Among the attributes that distinguish free people from property are that property can be transferred, acquired, owned. It can be given away. It can be collected. It is an it. In our culture, women carry a number of the attributes of property. In his excellent book, *The Gift*, Lewis Hyde observes that in our society some marriage ceremonies retain a vestige of a cultural tradition in which women are viewed as gifts of property. "Who giveth this woman?" the father is asked. The bride is given, for she is like property. No one gives the son, for he is not owned.

As women, we have in ancient times taken a seat as a near peer of commodities. A man counted among his wealth, say, his oxen, wheat, coins, and women. And though the giving of women—as in marriage—was not tantamount to the sale of property, the transfer was spiritually and to some extent legally inconsistent with a woman's fully realized self-ownership.

The concept of a woman as a thing acquired or acquirable perhaps has no more meaningful expression today than in the calm cultural acceptance—albeit with polite, mock disapproval—of the notion of wives as "trophies." At first a jarring social comment on the disposability of women, the phrase Trophy Wife now is used as a safe metaphor even for writers of established sensibilities and applied even to women who seem far too willful to be acquired. So it comes as no particular shock to see Jane Fonda, her previous political and commercial credits lovingly laid out like an exquisitely detailed bridal train, described recently in *Esquire* as a potential trophy wife for Ted Turner. And it comes as no surprise to see a winking television reporter comically juxtapose Donald Trump's description of the Plaza Hotel and other assets as "trophy properties" with a story about Trump's apparent pursuit of a younger, bouncier replacement wife.

Our status as near peers of property has had implications for our role in commerce. For the role of property owner seems more or less reserved for those who are themselves not property. Oxen do not, after all, have the legal right to own other oxen. And though, in this regard, a woman retained more legal property rights than non-humans—women have long been able to own estates and to bequeath them—many of her property rights dissolved into or became subject to the controlling legal rights of her husband upon marriage.

Women have emerged somewhat imperfectly from our erstwhile status as a near peer of property. There still remains a sense in the financial world that women are out of place in the world of money, despite the conspicuous examples of successful women managers. For example, the culture of bond trading, as Michael Lewis detailed in *Liar's Poker*, remains that of the "Big Swinging Dick." How you win at the game of finance is often still expressed in macho terms. You make a "killing" or "score" a win. To meet objectives, you are encouraged to "get the ball rolling." A particularly daring action shows you have "a lot on the ball" or, more tellingly, that you "have balls." Did you do well? Yeah, we "slaughtered 'em."

Once, in commenting on the adoption of certain guidelines tying the amount of reserves a bank must maintain to the riskiness of its portfolio, a man lamented privately, "Yeah, we [the United States] will obey these things, but Japan's going to rape the hell out of them." Again, the need to express an economic decision in terms excluding or demeaning to women seemed, to him, natural. The complaint he expressed was that the United States could not similarly rape the hell out of them. When he was challenged on his use of a metaphor, he indignantly complained, "Well, I just meant there wasn't a level playing field," itself a male-centric, though not patently offensive, form of sports-speak. This man's dilemma in finding a safe haven of metaphor is not unusual in that the general cultural themes of war and sport are at home in finance. And wherever women are in this language, we are not on the football field or the battlefield (at least we are not recognized as being there). We are essentially outside warrior-speak and sports-speak.

Some of you may object that women are not "outside" warrior-speak and sports-speak. True, women are as free as men to adopt the metaphors and culture of the battlefield and the playing field. Yes, we "score" and we "move the ball forward." But with one key difference. Men who adopt warrior-speak and sports-speak are, in some essential way, affirming this culture's view of maleness, giving the sign of the tribe. Until women are socialized on the battlefield and playing field, this affirmation, for women, is more an acknowledgment of the value of goal-orientation and aggressive pursuit of goals than an affirmation of tribal belonging.

Why Are the "Filthy Rich" Filthy?

Other contradictions and conflicts about money may be found in the subconscious, the domain of psychoanalysts. As you might expect, psychoanalysts have rather provocative views on why our financial behavior can be so complex.

Those building on the theories of Sigmund Freud, most notably Sandor Ferenczi, explain the human need to collect money as extending logically from the enjoyment we supposedly derive from our own feces. Basically the theory is that we so enjoyed our feces as infants that, throughout our lives, we continue to look for suitable substitutes. From feces, we move on to playing with mudpies, which have the desirable color and consistency and which are deodorized to boot, then on to sand, which represents an improvement over mud since sand does not stain our clothes, to collecting stones and pebbles, becoming "stone-rich," to colored marbles, to the final, fully-deodorized, unstaining form of feces—money. Thus, Freud and others in this school find it almost natural that, to use Freud's words, "Wherever archaic modes of thought have predominated or persist—in the ancient civilizations, in myths, fairy tales, and supersitions, in unconscious thinking, in dreams and in neuroses—money is brought into the most intimate connection with filth."

As amusing as the theory may seem, and as tempted as we may be to dismiss it as absurd, there are some startling historical connections between money and buttocks. K.F.

Flogel in his book *Geschichtedes Grotesk-Komischen* (as revised by Max Bauer) reports the following customs:

> In Naples, in former times, the insolvent debtor mounted a low pillar on the square in front of the Pazzo de' Tribunal (Palace of Justice) where he had to let down his pants, expose his naked bottom, and repeat three times: chi ha d'avere, si venga a pagare (Let all those whom I owe something come and collect!). This custom extended as far as Sicily.

> In Florence, insolvent debtors used to have to strike a large paving stone with their buttocks. This took place on the Mercato nuovo, with a crowd looking on. Through this act, they were freed of all pressure creditors might bring to bear on them. The custom is the source of the expression 'batter il culo sul lastrone', i.e., to become bankrupt.

> In the Netherlands, insolvent merchants had to sit down on a stone, their bottom[s] bare. In Swabia, in the village of Pfaffenhofen near Guglingen, a similar usage allegedly obtained.

Perhaps only a true Freudian can believe this unflinchingly. But we do not have to buy these theories wholesale to use them to advance our own explorations. For if in our subconscious and indeed our socialization we find the notion that "money is everything" sitting side by side with the notion that "money is dirty," is there any wonder that we are ambivalent about attaining money or keeping money? Is it at all surprising then that we feel money has no place on our hierarchy of values, yet we also judge ourselves privately by our ability to attain it? And is it surprising that the rich are at once admired and loathed?

We have conflicting views of money. In our heart of hearts we use it to measure our success in life, making its attainment a great, lifelong climb. Yet, having attained it, some have an insistent need to deny its meaning altogether.

How often we hear the multimillionaire smugly swear that, for all the millions tucked safely away, "I really don't care about money." And how often do we wish that we had so much money that we, too, could smugly deny its importance? In fact, our youth and middle years are a practical chase to obtain enough money so we can live our last years being just so smug.

How do we handle the continuous concern? How do we address a thing whose most lasting impression is its deeply felt absence?

Have you come to terms with money in your life? Or are you, like most of us, still at war with yourself because you don't have enough and can't figure out how to get more?

Reaching a truce with money, as you will see, really involves two goals. The first goal is to make peace with how much you have. This is a goal many wealthy or super wealthy people never attain, and as a result they never learn to enjoy their money, still are haunted by the prospect of poverty, still take stupid risks with their money. This is the reason multimillionaires can be caught cheating to save a few thousand dollars on taxes. They have no sense of proportion because they never answered the threshold question, "When is enough enough?" The second goal, for the millions who even with the best savings strategies still have insufficient funds, is to increase the amount of your discretionary net worth. The goal of this book is to help you accomplish both objectives. For reaching a truce with money has as much to do with how we feel about the weight of our purse as about the number of coins in our purse. It has as much to do with the qualities we, as women, bring to the task of reconciling resources with need as the fact that resources are limited. And so, we may ask at the outset, what qualities or habits do we have as women which may help or hinder our handling of the continuous concern that is money. Again, we needn't adopt the feces theory to know that a deep ambivalence about money can't be good for us, especially since we are continuously involved with the issue of money throughout our lives.

Impulses at War: When Your "Best" Instincts Can Hurt You

A singular source of conflict many women feel about money stems from the attempt to reconcile the financial demands of their roles as caretakers and nurturers with competing needs. Women historically have been and in large part continue to be socialized as caretakers. As caretakers, we are socialized to give our all to preserve the bonds of family. This caretaking includes financial giving where necessary. One of the first ways we practice nurturing is by caring for dolls. It is not difficult to remember such early nurturing feelings.

Stroking our doll's hair, we call her our baby and hug her close. We whisper in her plastic ears, "I love you." We imagine we see in her lifeless glass eyes that she loves us back. We are learning to take care of, to look after, to nurture.

She is only plastic, glass, and nylon. She cannot love us back. All the warmth we imagine she returns is really only our own love reflected in the glass eyes.

She cannot love us back. But we do not know this—not really—and we love her anyway, establishing an early pattern of investing our all-out giving to an object that cannot reciprocate. How many times will we repeat this empty pattern?

Behaviors repeated often enough can become habits. Habits repeated often enough can seem natural. And, decades after the little girl who saw love in lifeless eyes has forgotten the doll, the adult woman may find it natural to give all-out no matter what. She may find it natural to believe that underneath non-reciprocal relationships she is loved back:

She may look into lifeless eyes and see love.

She may regard lack of communication as silent strength.

She may give all, expect nothing, and yet feel natural.

She may have questions. But if she receives no answers to her questions, that's O.K., she knows how to supply the answers.

For dolls don't talk but they do love you back. Don't they?

Our socialization as all-out caregivers struggles against a basic current of money's flow. As trained caregivers, we have learned to put others at the centers of our lives.

Listen to the story of a little-known pioneer woman who died over a century ago, Eliza Donner:

Eliza Donner was one of the thousands of pioneer women who packed families into white, covered wagons, looking for all the world like white bonnets, to form a part of the 18th-century westward drive into unsettled territories of what was to become states such as Oregon and California. Many of these treks ended happily as families turned land into towns into states. But others, like the trek of the wagon train with the Donner family, ended tragically. Their march was halted midway by an unforgiving snowy winter. Oxen died, buffalo grew scarce for hunting, and the families rationed the remaining food. One mother felt fortunate to be able to feed each of her children a single square of tallow, pried from the trimmings of jerked beef. One of her children recalled that, "We nibbled off the four corners slowly, and then around and around the edges of the precious pieces until they became too small for us to hold between our fingers." Eventually, this kind of food, too, ran out. Some starved. In desperation, others turned to cannibalism.

The Donners were one of the families who refused to eat human flesh. Eliza's husband, George, grew ill. Finally, Eliza was presented with a choice of whether to try to move ahead to a post or stay behind. George was unfit to travel, and the choice Eliza faced amounted to whether to go ahead with her children and thus try to save herself also or stay with her husband and face almost certain starvation. As one of the survivors, Lewis Keseberg, recalls, Eliza followed instincts we have come to identify as "heroic": "She who had to choose between the sacred duties of wife and mother, thought not of self."

After her husband died in her arms, Eliza made a final trip in the snow to visit a man who had survived by eating flesh. With what must have been the last of her energy, she brought the man her life's savings to be given to her children, and she died later that night.

The ideal of ourselves as caregivers who put others at the centers of our lives becomes so deeply ingrained that it feels instinctive. It produces the voices teaching and constantly encouraging us to "think not of self," and creates the silent internal belief system we turn to reflexively in the middle of a crisis. In effect, it becomes our "best instinct."

But the money struggle is about keeping and investing. Its currents often pull in the opposite direction from the all-out giving central to caretaking and putting others at our centers. So a conflict builds. That conflict expresses itself, for example, in the large body of data chronicling the difficulty women have in performing the dual roles of full-time workers and the keepers of hearth and home. And we find that when it comes to money, our "best instincts" sometimes can hurt us.

The Stranger at the Center of Your Life

We are encouraged to put others at the centers of our lives. But the center only takes one occupant at a time. Only after others have taken their turns occupying our centers do some of us allow ourselves to move back in. "Now that the kids are all in college, I'm going to do things for myself," we assert. Or, "Now that Mom and Dad have passed away, I'm going to do for myself for awhile." Or, "Now that we are divorced, I'm going to please myself." Or, "Now that he's been unfaithful," and therefore, we reason, undeserving of our centers, we can slip back in. Implicit in the socialization that teaches us to put others at the centers of our lives is the notion that we, somehow, do not deserve to be there. Almost anyone or anything else will do. Husbands, children, the church, parents, jobs, country, name it. These are the things which, having occupied our centers, become our "reason for living." A woman who devotes herself to nurturing other occupants of her center is lavished with glowing adjectives: She is "generous," "big-hearted," "kind," and, best of all, "nice." She may be likened symbolically to Mary, the mother of Jesus, or to

Mother Earth. She is said to have a "heart of gold." But the woman (or man, for that matter) who occupies her own center or who appears to think more of herself than others is savaged with adjectives: She is "egotistical," "selfish," "self-centered," or "mean." She may be likened symbolically to a "witch" or a "dragon." She is said to have a "heart of stone."

Coming to terms with how our socialization as caretakers may work against us financially is difficult. Not all nurturing impulses are financially harmful. After all, caring for a business or taking charge of the family budget is a form of nurturing. But certainly the undifferentiating need to supply someone else's every need—including the need for money—and even at our own expense, does hurt us financially. The first financial task we face as adult women is somehow to reconcile the conflict between the all-out giving impulse fundamental to our role as caretakers and the keeping-in impulse necessary for financial growth. I suspect this inquiry will not produce clear-cut answers for any of us individually or for us collectively. Because the inquiry is multi-faceted, it is not simply reduced. It is not reducible, for example, to the mere rhetorical inquiry of whether "good mothers make bad savers." To be permanent or satisfying, the resolution of this inquiry must be informed at every step by our view of our roles in our families, in our extended family of friends, and in our society. This is our initial crossing.

Deciding to look at all critically at our socialization sets up painful conflict. After all, the all-out giving impulse is not appended to us like a scarf we can throw off. It is so deeply learned that it is integral. Still, we must decide what parts of that socialization to throw out, what parts to keep. We must, as well as we can, perform self-surgery. It will not be easy.

Changing Roles

Most of us have never tried to identify our relationship with money. Unconscious of patterns, uninformed and therefore unlearning, we retrace paths we swore we would never walk upon again. We are genuinely astonished at our own gullibility and naivete.

"At 30 years of age, I thought I'd never fall for that sob story again. Next time, I'm going to say 'no'," laments Mary, an attorney, as she retells the frustration of lending money to a friend who will not repay. Mary has unwittingly become her friend's banker, a convenient teller window when Susan is "short."

"When Susan and I were growing up, we were best friends. You know, we shared clothes...did each other's hair, promised to raise our kids next door to each other. I was always the better student, the dull one, and Susan was the artistic one. Then, dull me, I went off to college and law school and got a job that I hate some days and find rewarding other days, and, let's face it, it pays the bills. Susan went to drama school, and now she works as an aerobics instructor while she waits on her big break. When Susan runs out of money, she doesn't ask me, she doesn't have to ask—I just give it to her. She just kind of sits at my kitchen table and tells me her woes and leaves the silence between us. Then, before I know what I'm say-ing—I usually can't believe what I'm saying—I rush into the breach, offering a little money to tide her over. When Susan takes the money, she never promises to pay me back, and the funny thing is, I can't make myself ask her when she's going to pay me back. I guess I just hope she understands I'm not rich."

Mary, like many of us, has assumed a financial role she finds uncomfortable, even impossible at times, to fulfill. Over the years, Mary calculates she has lent Susan thou-sands of dollars under the vague unspoken understanding that a friendship based on love and trust somehow will force the money equation to balance out over the course of a lifetime.

But because the understanding is unspoken, it is likely that Mary and Susan have vastly different views of the terms of the understanding. To Mary, the terms of the understanding with Susan may be, "I'll help Susan now, and she'll pay me back later. And if and when her big break comes, I'll be the one who won't have to ask. She'll naturally cut me in on the money, the spotlight, and all the glorious rest." Susan, silent Susan, may understand only, "I have a great, generous friend, Mary, salt-of-the-earth, more like a mother than a friend, really. She's a true giver, never expects anything in return."

Little wonder that over the years Mary has grown increasingly resentful of what she sees as Susan's air of entitlement. But because she does not dare even to look at the underlying contract, she has no tools to re-order it, so she merely shrugs, mumbles something about "next time," and the problem grows. What keeps Mary from finding out the terms of the unspoken contract?

There is in each of our lives a hierarchy of people and concepts. Each of us has a different, personalized hierarchy, making up in effect a priority ladder. The different rungs on this hierarchical ladder may be religion, family, career fulfillment, self-preservation, pets, and, naturally enough, money. For example, a hypothetical hierarchy may be:

1. God

2. Spouse and children

3. Country

4. Health

5. Job

If asked to list the five most important things to them, most people would find it uncomfortable to list money among the top five, though certainly money is necessary for sustenance. Mary may have decided that her friendship with Susan ranks infinitely higher than money, and she may feel entirely comfortable saying that between Susan and her, money is "meaningless." But Mary's assessment that money is "meaningless" when compared to the value of Susan in her life is probably a dangerous exaggeration. We cannot say that money will rank ahead of Susan, but certainly money ranks far higher than the meaningless rung.

Mary's denial of the meaning and importance of money in sustaining her own life prevents her from honestly assessing her own needs. Perhaps a truer hierarchy for Mary is:

1. God
2. Self-preservation, which includes money necessary to sustain her life
3. Preservation of loved ones
4. Country
5. Job

What would happen if Mary were to acknowledge to herself that the long hours she spends in earning her money are meaningful and therefore worthy of respect? I suspect that such an acknowledgment, if repeated enough, would begin a gradual shift in the positions of the rungs on Mary's ladder of values, causing money to occupy a position closer to Mary's honest view of it. After all, few, if any of us can honestly say that money is "meaningless." For the overwhelming number of us, money and our relationship to it play a critical, though largely unexamined, role in shaping our lives.

The path now cluttered with ambivalence about whether having money or controlling money is an unwomanly or unfeminine thing impedes our ability to make good, hard, practical choices. We must begin to accept that we are, to a great degree, the architects of money's meaning in our lives. It does not need to be dirty. It does not need to be worshipped. It need only be accepted as a means of obtaining sustenance, occupying a high place, therefore, on our ladder of values, and managed accordingly.

part two:

PLANNING

5. Saving, Spending, Budgeting: Changing Your Relationship with Money

Most of us at some point in our lives have heard the old adage that money should be made to "work for you." But the many ways in which money can be invested may seem at times chaotic. Each year the list of investment products grows longer. A sample of the products reads like some hip, esoteric code decipherable only by investment bankers—CATS, TIGRS, zero convertibles, alphabet common.

Much of this razzle dazzle is designed more to show you how smart the jargonspeaker is than to communicate to you what is meant. The impulse to speak in undecipherable jargon comes from the same childish impulse to speak in pig Latin: "I eed-nay a ocolate-chay ookie-cay."

Beyond the mountain of jargon, however, what you discover is a reasonably simple array of investment choices. What you also discover is that the historical performances of certain investment products have been consistently better than others. In short, what you begin to see are money currents. And as your eyesight and financial habits improve, you steadily improve your ability to identify those currents that can indeed work for you and those that almost always work against you.

Improving Your Fitness as a Shopper: How to Detect Mental Blind Spots and Other Traits

But before we launch into an examination of the available products among which we can shop, we should first take a hard look at ourselves as shoppers. It is an important examination. For, as you will see, smart shopping ultimately depends as much on our fitness as shoppers before we even enter the store as on the product choices in the aisles.

First, we should check our eyes. The critical first question we ask is, "How do we perceive risk?" Though most financial advisers stress the importance of knowing how much risk we feel comfortable bearing for a given promise of return, few focus on the means we should use to assess risk. Fewer still focus on the mental habits we may have acquired that can distort our perception of risk.

Perception experts are making us more and more aware of certain "mental blind spots" that can distort our ability to make sound financial decisions. For example, one recent magazine piece asked readers to estimate the number of movie houses in the Soviet Union. Readers were asked to choose an estimated range broad enough for them to feel 90 percent sure that the correct number fell within that range. For example, you might be 90 percent sure that the correct number is between 10 and 50. What would you guess?

According to our perception experts, most of us try to answer this question by first deciding on a "right" answer, then stretching a band of uncertainty around the answer we have chosen.

The correct answer is 150,000. Was your guess close? The problem, it turns out, is that most of us do not discount enough for what we do not know. We forge ahead, making decisions based on amazingly few facts. Then we overcompensate for what we do not know—and here is the blind spot—by assuming that what we do not know is not important.

Other than our eyes, probably our second most important trait as shoppers is our "temperament." Webster's defines "temperament" as our "characteristic or habitual inclination or mode of emotional response" to an event. Are you by nature patient, measured, impetuous, daring, nervous, unflappable, stubborn? Success in investing requires, more than any other trait, the ability to follow through on a strategy once you have chosen one. It requires patience. Jumping in and out of strategies and constantly changing directions midstream is a trick only the luckiest among us can perform consistently without disaster. For most of us, a winning strategy is accomplished only by sifting through what we know—and do not know—and by being patient enough to let the plan work.

A third shopping trait we should examine closely is our affinity for bright lights and noise. Early on, we learn the allure of spectacle. A shout of "Fight!" pulled us as children away from the most loved project and drew us to the edge of crowds, straining our necks to get a glimpse of spectacle. Or, asked to choose a toy, we grabbed the one colored sunshine yellow or fire-engine red. Likewise, when it comes to investments, we stampede toward the latest go-go. In the '60s, anything with a high-tech name would do. As the late Benjamin Graham, a brilliant investment strategist, has noted, shrewd companies soon caught on to our fondness for high-tech sounding names, and some kept their old product lines, merely changed their names, and saw their profits grow.

Though with maturity we have learned that the loudest mouth is not always the one worth listening to and that taupe or teal blue sometimes are preferable to fire-engine red, curiously the same kind of evolution does not readily occur when it comes to making investment decisions. Somehow we still think the company making the loudest noise or with the glitziest color is the best. We shun the drab for the dazzling, forgetting each time that a dollar produced by a toilet seat manufacturer's stock buys just as much as one from the stock of a state-of-the-art computer company.

Another internal check we should make is how we feel about spending money and about saving money. First, let's consider how we feel about saving money.

Dietitians have developed a theory to explain why people who diet tend to return to roughly the same weight time and time again. The central concept of the theory is that each of us has a "set point," an intrinsic thermostat determined by our metabolic rate. Trying to change our set point merely by making changes in diet, the theory goes, is doomed to fail, unless we also change our basic metabolic rate through exercise. I have begun to believe that each of us also has a "money set point." Our money set point is reflected in the amount of savings and net worth we feel comfortable having. If we acquire savings beyond this money set point, we begin to feel uncomfortable, and we may splurge on a shopping spree or vacation until we have whittled down our savings again to our set point. I have seen or read of examples of this phenomenon in the lives of many people. One friend believes that if she has $1,000 in the bank, she is fine, sufficiently "safe" from disaster. If a fairy godmother deposited $10,000 magically into her savings account, there is no doubt that my friend would find some way to spend or give away $9,000, returning her once again to the psychic comfort zone of her money set point. Perhaps the same phenomenon is at work in the surprisingly large numbers of stories reported about the unshakable bad money habits of some lottery winners. Suddenly rich, they find ways to outspend fortunes they never dreamed of having, returning once again to a level of relative poverty.

"Burning a hole in your pocket" is the way my great grandmother described an inability to save, to leave money alone. The quarter feels unusually heavy in a pocket accustomed to a nickel, every now and then a dime. The cotton pocket of my dungarees (they didn't become jeans until I became a teenager) actually seemed to sag, and I can remember impatiently wanting, needing to run to the store and buy twice the usual allotment of cookies.

Do You Feel You Deserve Less?

How much savings you feel comfortable having often veils a deeper question: How much money do you believe you deserve to have? For, if money has in our subconscious murky connections with feces and dirt, we cannot expect comfortably to associate saving money with the loftier sense of self we consciously link to self-worth. And yet, the link plainly is there, since we measure our life's worth so often by the financial success we achieve. And *self-worth* and *net-worth*, throughout our lives, continually play competing sisters in a drama of ambivalence.

We venture tentatively into savings plans, almost committing, then pulling back, subconsciously believing that saving beyond a certain point lands us too far from ourselves, maybe too far away from—or too close to—home. Too far away from or too close to mother's ways or father's ways. And did you swear that you would outperform them both? Or did you swear always to follow their footsteps, matching your steps with each footprint they left? Or were you determined to sweep away their footprints and make yours so new, so different? In either case, whether you are determined to imitate them or determined not to imitate them, your view of how much you should have, how much this world owes you, is shadowed by those parental footprints.

"My mother could never save a dime," Linda, a computer analyst, recalls. "If I needed money for a school project, it was never there." Linda remembers. You can hear the pain in her voice even now, forty years after the money for that school project was not there. For her own two children, Linda planned years ahead, becoming almost obsessed with planning. She delayed having the first child until well into her thirties, until she "was set," so determined was she that her children "would never have to worry." She is determined not to match the footprints before her.

Learning the Fine Art of Haggling

We should also, finally, check our ability and willingness to negotiate. Information on the ability and willingness of women to haggle is sparse and somewhat inconsistent, with one report by the American Council of Life Insurance suggesting that women comparison shop more than men while other reports suggest that women lag behind men in negotiating skills. What is clear, however, is that women are treated far differently from men by sellers of certain major products. In fact, the alarming truth is that for many big ticket items, women literally are paying a gender tax.

Take cars, for example. After the home, cars represent the single biggest lifetime purchase for most people. But a recent American Bar Foundation study found that car dealerships give substantially better "final offers" on car prices to men than women. Examining the practices of over 400 car dealerships in the Chicago area, the study revealed that the average final offer to men on a car with a dealer sticker price of $13,465 was $11,362. The dealer's cost of the car, including air conditioning and power steering, was $11,000. The final offer to women, by contrast, averaged $11,504, *representing an increase of 40 percent in the markup over the price offered to men.*

A significant part of the results are attributable to the perception on the part of dealers that women have less developed bargaining skills than men. How we feel about haggling can mean the difference between getting a fair price for a car or other good and, literally, being taken for a ride.

If we assume that car dealers are not unique in their low opinion of the negotiating skills of women—a safe assumption—then, in many cases, women probably pay significantly more than men for those goods with negotiable prices. When you add up the costs of housing, cars, and other big ticket items women buy over the course of a lifetime, the unwillingness to haggle and the gender tax may cost you hundreds of thousands of dollars in lost savings.

How do you learn to haggle? Well, as with most other skills, you learn mostly by practicing. But here are a few tricks of the trade that can shorten your learning time:

- Set goals before you start to haggle. Don't go into a negotiation with the vague objective of "getting all you can." The danger of this approach is that you may lose sight of when you have won. And once you lose sight of when you have won, you may fight longer than you must and cause the seller to break the deal. Also, knowing how far you want to go will give you a clear idea of how much you can give up.

- Never start haggling until you have convinced yourself that you do not need the product or service. You know what makes successful negotiators successful? It is the ability to convey that they want it less than you. Or look at it another way. The person who wants it more will give up more to get it. If you give off the unmistakable smell of desperation, you will get taken—period. So cover that scent, sweeten it with the perfume of indifference, even if you really want the car, house, whatever. For the millisecond you start thinking thoughts like "Oh, but I really want it," and "I can't let this one get away from me," you begin in effect to transfer dollars from your pocket to the seller's.

- Use time as a weapon. If at all possible, let the seller do the calling, writing, and courting. Take as much time to make up your mind as you can. Knowing how much time you have is an art, and you will get better as you haggle more.

- Show the seller your back at least once in every negotiation. I first learned this trick while in college during a trip to Morocco at a—where else—bazaar. If you turn your back and pretend to walk away, you send a message clearer than any number of words, that you, not the seller, own the bargaining power. Do not overuse this trick, and when you turn away, be prepared truly to leave. For this reason, it is best to save this for when things look truly bad. You can, for example, turn your back figuratively by failing to call the seller at a scheduled time or by telling the seller you will sleep on an offer overnight and get back to him or her in the morning.

• Never impugn the integrity of the person with whom you are negotiating to gain an edge. Before you call someone a "liar" or a "cheat," you ought to believe what you are saying. And if you believe what you are saying, you ought not to be in the process of concluding a deal with that person.

The techniques above will help you improve your ability to save. But saving is only half the story. Listen, also, to how you feel about spending.

What Your Feelings About Shopping Reveal About You

How you feel about spending may be largely revealed in your view of shopping. For what you spend your money to buy reflects in large part what you feel are necessities. Though some social planners feel that they know what is "necessary" for all of us, each of us is free to make up our own list of those things we absolutely must have. And though food, clothes, shelter, transportation, and medical care constitute an average array of necessities, some may believe that silk pajamas or chocolate fudge make life worth living. Beyond whatever you call necessities, there are, of course, other things to do with your money. Some, maybe legions, are disciples of shopping for its own sake.

To them, shopping is a calling. It is a way to transform money earned in unglamorous, perhaps unworthy pursuits into, well, a Ming vase or Chanel necklace. It turns bootlegged whiskey into a university library.

Shopping is self-love. Shopping for the working woman may be a way to reward herself, lavish herself with love. It is a self-massage.

Shopping is a thrill. It is the power to spend. Women not only buy women's clothes but 60 percent of men's ties also. I have felt the thrill. After spending for necessities and on everyone else, I sometimes enjoy indulging for its own sake. Rosettes on my wall's border and broccoli florets on my omelette and all the little things, berber carpet and mother-of-pearl lights and every little thing I could never care about when I had too many cares were now mine for the buying and the fussing over. And I bought and fussed over them all with the relish of a dry-mouthed drunkard's splash in a sea of wine.

How we feel about spending influences how we feel about saving. For spending is just the flip side of saving. If we care only about spending, we may view saving as an annoying intrusion on our God-given right to shop. And if we care only about saving, we may view spending as a moral evil. Both roads lead to hell.

Savings Strategies That Work

The most effective way to save is to allocate a certain amount each month for saving and a certain amount for splurging. Pay yourself right off the top before you pay any other bills. I know many of you are smiling now—what does she mean, pay myself, I can't find enough to pay my existing bills! But the fact is, our budgets tend to expand or contract to fit our habits. Remember the example of the lottery winners who find ways to spend millions they never dreamed of having. Remember the times when you were hit with an unexpected expense and somehow found the money. Or remember when you really wanted to take that trip or plan for that big wedding or buy that perfect gift. The money somehow appeared. If you treat your savings as just another bill, you will be amazed at how you will find ways to pay yourself.

Think of it as a self-bill. Make the self-bill equal to your average monthly phone bill or laundry bill or food bill for starters, then increase the self-bill every six months or so. It will begin to add up.

To make it even more realistic, type up an invoice to yourself, make twelve copies, put them in a self-addressed stamped envelope, and have a friend mail one to you each month. When you get the self-bill, pay it within five days by depositing that amount in a special savings account just for this purpose, and charge yourself a fee of $5 if you pay late. The form on the next page can be a starting model for your self-bill.

Once you begin to pay your self-bill regularly, give yourself a rebate of one month's installment for every six months of timely payments. Then, use that rebate to splurge on something to pamper yourself. The pampering, maybe a pedicure or a facial or a dinner at your favorite restaurant—use your imagination—will make the next self-bill seem easier to pay.

Another effective way to save is never to see your money. Many people find that the best way to save is to have a certain amount automatically deducted from their paychecks before they receive them. The rationale is that by having the money out of your immediate grasp, you remove the temptation to spend, and it seems to work. You may set up automatic deduction plans through your employer, through your bank or even certain mutual funds, such as the Janus Fund.

The basic rationale of the automatic account builder— what you do not see, you do not spend—can be applied in other ways. For example, many people have improved their savings habits using bank certificates of deposits (CDs). The idea is to buy three-month or six-month CDs with as much of your disposable cash as you can spare. As these mature, buy additional short-term CDs as frequently as your income permits. Since most CDs are cashable only at maturity—or a stiff penalty is assessed—putting into CDs the cash that you would ordinarily leave lying around in a savings account makes the cash less accessible. At least, it feels less accessible, and that is the key psychological benefit of saving this way.

Of course, you could use any number of investment products in this way. The only constraint is the minimum amount of money required to buy the product and whether

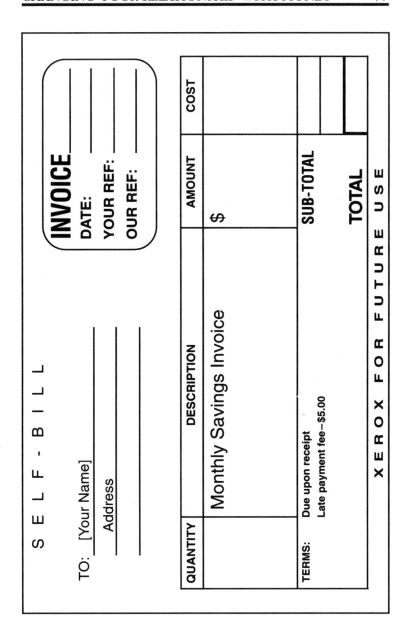

Figure 5-1

the product is short-term. You would not want to tie up all your spare cash long-term in case of emergencies.

Improving Your Money Awareness: "Where Does All My Money Go?"

The following exercise is designed to help you improve your awareness of how and why you spend your money. It is not a "test" because there are no right and wrong answers. Instead, this exercise will sensitize you to how you view money and how that view may be helping or hindering your efforts to reach a comfortable balance between spending and saving. Answer these questions when you are alone. Since no one is peering over your shoulder to judge your saintliness, answer the questions as fearlessly as possible.

1. How would you complete the following sentence: "If I had_____in my hands right now, I could pretty much solve all my money problems."

2. You have a choice of spending $100 to buy a present for your mother which she does not need or putting $100 in a savings account for yourself. Which are you likely to do?

3. The same question as in (2) but the choice is between a present for your spouse or significant other and yourself?

4. The same question as in (2) but the choice is between your child and yourself?

5. You are earning $20,000 per year. Your spouse earns $50,000 per year. If you could determine your future and his, would you rather (a) always make less than he makes, (b) make about the same as he makes or (c) outearn him by a substantial margin? How would your answer change if you were to substitute your best friend for your spouse in this question?

6. Your adult son was educated as a lawyer but has discovered that the law gives him ulcers and has decided he would rather not work for an indefinite period to recuperate. How would you feel about supporting him financially for one year? For three years? Indefinitely?

7. Same question as (6) but what conditions, if any, would you place on his receipt of the money?

8. You and your roommate share living expenses. But lately she has been a few days late in paying her share of the phone bill. Do you feel comfortable asking her to make timely payments? Would you hesitate before talking with her about it? Would you worry whether she would think you were cheap?

9. You have been doing stellar work at your job, but you have not received a promotion for several promotion cycles. Do you feel comfortable discussing the matter with the powers-that-be?

10. Your sister is dying of a rare form of cancer which, with extraordinary medical care, gives her only a one-in-ten chance of survival. Unfortunately, she does not carry insurance to cover the treatment and has asked you to help financially. How much money are you willing to give? Would your answer depend on whether the amount in question represents a significant part of your net worth? Would your answer be any different if her chances of survival were nine-in-ten with treatment?

11. Assuming most health insurance policies would cover the treatment, would your answer to (10) change if you had been asking, even begging, your sister for years before she became ill to get adequate insurance?

12. How much money do you think you would need to make each year to live comfortably?

13. Complete this statement: There are some things money cannot buy, including _____.

14. Complete this statement: There are some things money cannot buy, but for $1,000,000 I would:

    (a) agree never to set foot in a church again

    (b) give up my citizenship

    (c) shorten my life by one year

    (d) divorce

    (e) agree never to marry

    (f) insert any of the items listed in (13)

    (g) none of the above

15. Complete this statement: Before I die, I'd like to earn $ _____ and have a net worth of $ _____.

16. Which of the following persons are you most likely to tell your salary: (a) your co-worker, (b) your high school buddies, (c) a stranger.

17. Assume that for a ten-year period you could earn 10 percent on average a year if you invest in stocks and you could earn 5 percent on average a year if you kept your money in a bank. If you have $100,000 to spend, how much of it would you invest in stocks? How much in the bank? How would your answer change if you had only $1,000 to invest?

18. You are 24 and you have the rare gift of being able to see the future. You are in love with Mr. Y, but you see he will never amount to much. In fact, your financial life with him would be hell. He would make at maximum only $3,500 per year and you would have to work three jobs to support the family. Mr. W's future on the other

hand shows he will become a millionaire, but you have only lukewarm feelings for him. Do you (a) marry Y, (b) marry W, (c) marry W but have an affair with Y, (d) none of the above?

19. Would your answer be different if your daughter were selecting among eligible partners presenting the same choices?

20. Take out a dollar bill. Would you feel comfortable burning it? If not, do you view burning money as a sin? If so, against whom is it a sin— God, humanity, the country, yourself?

21. You have just won $1,000 in the lottery. Do you intend to save all of it? What amount of it?

22. Same question as in (21) but you earned the extra $1,000 by working overtime.

23. Your friend Jo borrowed $100 from you and repaid you with a check. The check bounced. Do you feel comfortable confronting Jo about the check? Do you feel comfortable asking Jo to pay for any bank charges you may incur if you have written other checks against the bounced check?

24. You borrowed $100 from your friend Jo and promised to repay it in a month. The month is almost up and you find you do not have the money. When do you let Jo know? How do you let Jo know? Also, would you be more likely to borrow from Jo if you knew she made (a) twice as much as you, (b) one-half what you do, or (c) about as much as you do?

25. If you knew you would never earn any more money than you do now, could you be happy?

The payment of self-bills, automatic account builders, and the Money Awareness Exercise are three tools you can use to begin to strike a workable balance between saving and spending. But after you have saved a bit, what do you invest in? And how much should be invested in each product? The next several chapters should give you a more detailed understanding of the array of investment products available and how they differ. Later in this chapter, we develop an investment profile for women at various stages of life, from their twenties to their nineties. We then explore how to allocate assets effectively to fund special financial risks you face in each of the stages of your life. Then, we discuss in more detail the risk and reward characteristics of various investment products.

Developing Your Risk Profile

True or false: A man and woman of the same age, earning the same wage, have identical risk profiles. Many financial planners, perhaps most, would answer this question with an unqualified "true." But, for reasons given below, I believe that women should allocate their assets in a significantly different way from men.

At the threshold, we may ask what qualities distinguish women from men as investors? Are women greater risk-takers than men or are we more risk-averse? Are we more likely to comparison shop? To seek advice? Are women more or less concerned than men about the need for financial planning?

The answers, as revealed through research by various organizations, present an interesting puzzle. It turns out that women are far more concerned than men about the need for financial planning. Women also are more likely than men to seek advice and to comparison shop. However, the data also shows that women are more risk-averse than men. When asked the question, "Are you willing to take some risks for a chance to realize greater investment gains?" only 38 percent of women surveyed by the American Council of Life Insurance answered "yes." In contrast, 48 percent of men would take more risks to earn greater investment gains.

Consistent with being relatively risk-averse, women are more likely than men to trust and to rely on bank accounts as the principal vessel for savings, and women expressed a relative distrust of brokerage houses. The women surveyed believe as many as 41 percent of all stockbrokers are incompetent. Women also are less likely than men to be familiar with a broad range of investment products. A full 50 percent of women surveyed reported that they "Keep most of their money in banks because they don't know about other investments." These results have adverse implications for the ability of women effectively to allocate assets to manage increased life risks, such as becoming principal providers of eldercare and childcare and outliving retirement savings.

What emerges from a review of the results is paradoxical. Women need more money to fund special life risks but are less likely to take on added investment risk for a chance to earn the higher investment returns. We know we need more money but are unwilling to invest strategically to get it. We are willing to seek out advice but do not trust the competence of those offering it. Because there is no getting around the critical need for effective asset allocation, the only practical option remaining for those of us who need advice but do not trust others to do our investing, is to learn as much as we can about sound investment allocation so that we can, in effect, do it ourselves.

Putting the Right Number of Eggs in the Right Baskets

"Don't put all your eggs in one basket," as my grandmother warned, is probably the best way to express the fundamental concept behind asset allocation: assets should be spread around to diversify risk. Then, if one basket should fall to the ground, breaking all the eggs inside, you have others to count on.

Effective allocation of assets, as a general matter, depends on the evaluation of (1) the inherent risk an asset carries and (2) the rate of return required to meet your needs. Because of their structure and lack of guaranteed return, some assets are inherently riskier to own than others. At the safest end of the continuum are products such as various United States government securities, certain corporate bonds, and, of course, cash. Somewhere in the middle of the continuum are certain stocks of large companies that have performed well for many years (blue-chip stocks) and certain mutual funds. At the very riskiest end of the continuum are products such as the stocks of start-up companies, high-yield (junk) bonds, certain derivative products (such as stripped securities), and certain types of limited partnerships, such as those that invest in oil and gas exploration. As you go from the safest to the riskiest end of the continuum, the rate of return increases. This conclusion, roughly borne out empirically, is sometimes stated in expressions such as that "risk and return are tradeoffs" or are "inversely related." You can ask the key question in two ways. How much risk are you willing to bear for the potential return? Or how much return would you require for the risk the investment carries?

What is clear is that to meet our special financial needs, women must diversify holdings to some degree both to counteract the effects of inflation and to take advantage of the ability of products like stocks to deliver returns superior to cash over longer periods. Left in cash form under a mattress, your portfolio would dwindle to nothing in little time. This is true for any significant period during this century.

For example, how much would $1 invested at year-end 1925 grow to be by year-end 1987? Roger Ibbotsen of Ibbotsen Associates has answered that question for four assets: common stocks, small-company stocks, long-term (20-year), high-grade corporate bonds, long-term government bonds, intermediate-term (at least five years) government bonds, and United States Treasury bills:

Asset	*Value*
common stocks	$347.00
small-company stocks	$1,202.97
long-term corporate bonds	$19.78
long-term government bonds	$13.52
intermediate-term government bonds	$17.89
United States Treasury bills	$8.37

During this same sixty-two-year period, an average 3 percent inflation rate made $1 equal to $6.44. So, as you can see, after adjusting for inflation, some investments, particularly T-bills, were barely profitable. And $1 kept under a mattress would have lost almost all its value by 1987.

It is clear that the products with greater potential to deliver superior investment returns also carry higher risks. How much risk you are willing to bear for a given potential return is a personal choice. To make this evaluation, you should take a hard look at your personal needs. At the outset, you should recognize that your investment needs change depending on your age, your earnings potential, and, as we have seen, your sex, as well as a number of other factors. Creating a profile of your investment needs at various stages of your life has spawned an entire industry of financial advisers. What all reputable advisers have in common is an attentiveness to how your profile differs from that of other investors and a willingness to explain the methodology to you until you understand it.

An Allocation Strategy for Women: The Modified Pyramid

Once you have identified your current assets, using the forms in Appendix A, we can allocate what percentage of your assets should be kept in each form.

We will be using a "pyramid" strategy. Following this strategy will help you build up net worth in a relatively safe, controlled manner while also giving you a reasonable shot at good long-term gains. The pyramid strategy recognizes that a sound investment strategy must balance four goals: liquidity, safety, income, and capital appreciation. In this sense, the pyramid works as a sound strategy for all investors, not only women.

But the pyramid should be modified further for women. The typical allocation profile depends on your age, number of dependents, and net worth. Generally speaking, as your age increases, the amount of payment risk in your portfolio should decrease. You should allocate a greater share of your portfolio to riskier investments (meaning products other than cash, near-cash, and investment-grade bonds) during your twenties and thirties, no more than half your portfolio to such products during your forties, and no more than 15 percent of your portfolio during your fifties and sixties. During your seventies, eighties and nineties (yes, some of you will get there), no more than 1 percent of your portfolio should be allocated to such products. It bears repeating that the risk being decreased is payment risk. Other types of risk, for example, the risk of inflation eroding your cash and near-cash assets, remain.

Planning for Your 20s, 30s, 40s, 50s, 60s and Beyond

The typical investment allocation strategies do not fit most women. Women, for the reasons identified earlier, are much more likely than men to face certain financial challenges and risks and have fewer resources to fall back on if the strategy fails. We have weaker safety nets. As a result, a risk allocation that does not take into account a woman's increased chance of becoming the principal provider of eldercare and childcare, her increased need for retirement income stream because she outlives men, and the other special risks she faces is ineffective. To adjust for the increased chance of encountering these risks and the more gossamer or non-existent safety net women have, the allocation picture should be adjusted in the following manner.

First, in her twenties, when she has the best chance of taking advantage of the long-term upward trend of blue-chip common stocks, she should have higher percentages of her net worth in such products than men. If it is reasonable for a man in his twenties making $25,000 to $40,000 to have between 50 percent and 70 percent of savings in stocks, then a woman should have between 60 and 80 percent of her allocation in stocks. The bigger rates of return stocks traditionally have produced will help fund her longer retirement income stream needs. In her thirties, the percentage should not fall below 50 percent and can range as high as 70 percent of her portfolio. One important point to note is that, until she is fifty-nine-and-a-half or near

retirement, she should not change her allocations by cashing out securities; rather her allocation should be changed
by funneling new dollars saved into lower risk categories.
For example, if you are 29 and have a stock allocation percentage of 80 percent—acceptable for a woman in her
twenties—you should not cash out 10 percent of your stock
to bring your allocation down before your thirtieth birth-
day. Instead, you should decrease the percentage allocable
to stocks by increasing the amount of new dollars put in a
lower risk category, such as bank CDs.

The strategy must change for women in their thirties,
however, to begin to prepare for the risk of becoming the
principal providers of eldercare. If we assume your parents
are at least twenty years older than you, then they will be
entering their fifties as you enter your thirties.
Geriontologists estimate that the onset of debilitating illness
occurs most often between the ages of 65 and 85, so our
hypothetical parent still has fifteen years before the risk of
becoming dependent becomes significant. During this
fifteen-year period, and assuming you would choose to
shoulder this obligation, you should allocate at least 5 percent of your stock portfolio to cover the costs of eldercare.
This 5 percent should not increase the overall recommended range, so that if, for example, you are at 70 percent
already, you should not invest in an extra 5 percent simply
to fund this eldercare protection. And even after accounting
for the 5 percent devoted to eldercare, your remaining percentage of assets devoted to stocks is still higher than the
general investor's.

The drawing in Figure 5-2B represents a pyramid modified for a woman in her twenties, thirties, and forties.
Figure 5-2C shows the pyramid as it should appear for a
woman in her fifties, sixties, and seventies, the years when
the percentage of stocks and other equities held should
decrease, and the percentages of cash and fixed-income
products, such as bonds and CDs, should increase. In
Figure 5-2D the pyramid reflects the proper percentages
of risk for a woman in her eighties and nineties.

As you can see, the pyramid is divided into three hori-
zontal slices. Because of the shape of the pyramid, the sec-

tions get progressively smaller as you go up. Let's take an example to show you how to interpret the table's drawings. If you are a woman in your thirties, the base third of the pyramid, the broadest section, will constitute disproportionately more of your available savings, approximately 50 percent to 70 percent. The base section is assigned the task of meeting the goal of capital appreciation. It will be used for long-term funding needs, such as retirement, eldercare, and college costs and will be invested in a combination of blue-chip stocks and growth-oriented mutual funds, variable annuities, and, to a lesser extent, real estate. Because these types of investments grow fastest in value over time, they also act as natural hedges against inflation. Determine the amount you will put in your base third before you move up the pyramid.

The second section makes up between 20 percent and 45 percent of your portfolio and will be used to achieve the goal of income generation. The bonds, money-market funds and accounts, and related products that will make up this slice, though they produce no capital appreciation, are relatively free of payment risk and produce a fairly high income stream.

The tip of the pyramid, for most of your life, will constitute the smallest share of your overall portfolio, accounting for between 5 and 10 percent. This slice is made up of mostly cash and, to a lesser extent, near-cash products.

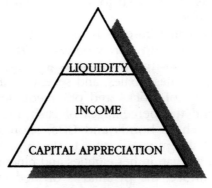

Figure 5-2A

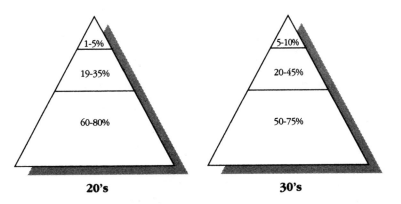

20's   **30's**

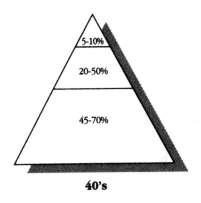

40's

Figure 5-2B

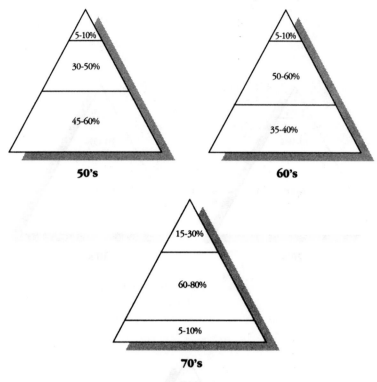

Figure 5-2C

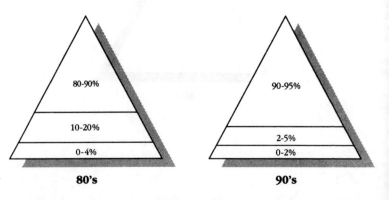

Figure 5-2D

6. The Risk Return Tradeoff: How Much Risk Should You Bear?

In our modified pyramid strategy, we ordered investment products according to how risky they are. In this chapter, we will examine more closely how to arrive at a determination of a product's inherent riskiness. Because risk is a tradeoff to return, a good rule of thumb to remember is that as the investment gets riskier, you may lose sleep, but if the investment works out, you may wake up far richer. The corollary rule is that with the safer investments, you will get a better night's sleep, but you have a lesser chance of waking up rich in the morning. So, one way to look at the basic issue of investment choice is—how much is a good night's sleep worth to you?

To see how risk and return are inextricably related, consider the following choices. You are given the chance to invest $1 on the chance to earn $1,000,000 in a state lottery with only 100 people participating. Each participant therefore has a 1 in 100 chance of winning. Should you do it? Most of us would not hesitate to jump in. To analyze why we would not hesitate is intriguing. We begin to evaluate a potential investment by first assessing the potential harm or "downside." The bigger the downside we face, the bigger the upside needed to entice us to jump in. Here, the downside is minimal—only $1. Because the downside is almost negligible, we do not fear making the investment, and the upside potential needed to entice to gamble can be quite small. Most of us would lose no sleep risking the dollar for a chance to earn $500,000, $1,000 or even $100. In fact, as long as the size of the investment is negligible relative to our net worth, we lose no sleep. And since to most of us $1 is a negligible investment, we consider the consequence of losing the dollar miniscule. Notice that in this example, we are examining only one kind of risk, the risk measured by the size of our investment relative to our personal financial resources.

Now, change the example, and make the minimum investment $10,000 for a chance to earn $1,000,000. With this amount at stake, many more of us would balk, scratch our chins and look the investment over far more carefully. We would hesitate, even though the objective chance of winning the jackpot has not changed. It is still 1 in 100. We would hesitate because the personal risk we face if the investment does not pan out, if something goes wrong, would hurt us deeply financially. And if we took the gamble, the night before the lottery drawing would be a restless one.

But what if the number of participants shrinks? What if, instead of 100 participants in the lottery, there were only two? Now, even though your personal stake is $10,000, the chance for upside is enormous, a fifty-fifty chance to win $1,000,000. Now would you risk it? Many more of us would.

All Risks Are Not the Same

What these examples show is that the lottery and, indeed, most investments present at least two kinds of risk. First, there is the risk inherent in the game itself. For the lottery that risk depends on the number of people playing. If only one person plays, there is no risk, and you have no chance of losing. If one billion people play, you have almost no chance of winning. Second, there is the risk measured by how much the stake means to us personally. If your net worth is $10,000, an investment of $10,000 means the world to you while the same investment may seem riskless to a billionaire. Our perception of risk increases as the potential jackpot gets smaller.

Conversely, our perception of risk decreases as the jackpot gets bigger. That is, for the same amount of investment, we perceive less risk in playing a game where the jackpot is $1,000,000 as opposed to a game where the jackpot is $1,000. This is true even though the objective risk, measured for example by the number of players in a lottery, remains the same.

As a general matter, we demand a higher potential jackpot—return—as the objective or personal risk of an investment increases.

You may have wondered just how profitable (or risky) certain common investments are compared with others. The S&P 500 index for the decade of the 1980s shows that during the 1980s, stocks experienced a broad growth, averaging about 15 percent. During that same period, taxable corporate bonds averaged 12 percent return on investment. The top twenty growth mutual funds had growth paralleling that of the S&P 500, an unsurprising result since many of these funds invest in the same stocks that are used for the S&P 500. Bank passbook savings accounts averaged about 5 percent. The table on the next page compares the experience of certain investment products for the period from 1960 to 1984. (Certain products are not included because they didn't exist over the entire period researched.)

As the numbers show, the highest returns during the bull market were achieved by stocks and by mutual funds investing in stocks. During bear markets, bonds are generally the top performers. The same pattern of performance would be shown if we were to examine any of the other strong bull markets during the sixty-year period, such as the period from 1960–1970, the so-called "go-go" '60s period. The moral of the story? Stocks should be a part of a sound long-term portfolio, such as one geared to fund retirement, college costs, or other long-term goals. The earlier you begin to invest, the better, since the younger you

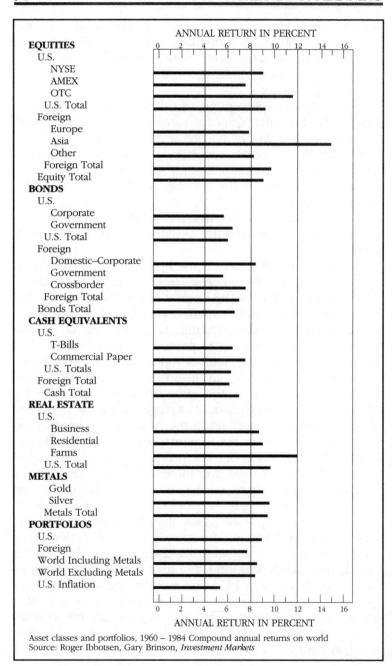

Asset classes and portfolios, 1960 – 1984 Compound annual returns on world
Source: Roger Ibbotsen, Gary Brinson, *Investment Markets*

Table 6-1

are, the more likely you are to experience several strong bull markets. Bonds, on the other hand, are useful for the production of income during bearish times and for those investors who are not likely to see as many bull markets.

The above answers the question of how much reward you can reasonably expect for certain products. It does not, however, tell us whether the reward we obtain is commensurate with the risk each product presents. To answer this question, we must more finely define what we mean by "risk." There are at least two types of inherent risk. There is the risk that you will lose your investment. This risk we have been referring to as a payment risk. Over the short-term there is also a kind of risk associated with volatility of the product—is the product likely to experience wild swings in value? The jitteriness of a product, even one performing well over the long-term, may make it unsuitable for your stomach if not your pocketbook. When most financial advisers speak of risk, they are really referring to payment risk. But when many investors speak of risk, they may mean both kinds of risk; they are concerned both about the eventual return of their money and a good night's sleep.

With respect to the jitteriness of a product, such as stock, we would expect that the most jittery stocks should return higher profits than the calm, steady-as-you-go performers to compensate for the higher gastronomic aggravation in holding these products. But mathematicians who have plotted the second type of risk for a broad-based portfolio have made a startling discovery: Jittery stocks do not over the long-term perform significantly better than their calmer cousins. What is the bottom-line? Since the market does not pay you more for holding jittery products, you should adjust your valuation of these products downward, as a general matter.

What about payment risk? Does the market pay you more in rate of return to compensate you for holding products with higher payment risk? The answer here is generally yes. As a general matter, stocks or other products that have higher chance of loss of invested capital do, as we have seen, have higher than average rates of return over the long term.

Because women historically have been more risk-averse than men, we may resist making the smartest long-run investment choices. It is smarter to invest long-term in stocks and mutuals. But because we fear both payment risk and jitteriness, we may be hesitant to make that move. The consequence can be very unfavorable for our long-term funding needs such as retirement, eldercare, and college costs. For, as we have seen, if we objectively evaluate the financial life risks women face compared to men, the conclusion we reach is that women should invest more aggressively than men, not less. It is especially unfortunate that we so often mix the two types of risks together in making an investment choice, since only one of them, payment risk, presents an objective danger to our portfolio strategy.

Where Are Women in the Stock Market?

In light of the fairly substantial data suggesting that women are more risk-averse than men, we would expect to find relatively small numbers of women stockholders. But in fact, the opposite is true. According to a New York Stock Exchange survey, women outnumber men as stockholders. What's going on? Yes, women, it turns out, represent about 51.5 percent of all stockholders. But most of these women received their stock not through actively acquiring it, but through gift or inheritance. By contrast, men are far more likely to have gone out and acquired stock as a result of investment choice. And, the women who own these stocks represent a small stratum of American women. Only 12.5 percent of all single female-heads of households (and 24 percent of all married couples) surveyed by the Census Bureau reported owning stock.

Moreover, there is a significant story behind the profile of those women who do own stock. These women tend to be older, and they tend to be widows. The 20 million women who own stock are on an average almost 49 years old, compared to the average age of male stockholders, 44. Women stockholders are more likely to live alone and to have acquired the stock through gift or inheritance from deceased husbands. In other words, the way they acquired the stock does not reflect a conscious planning ahead. More importantly, women stockholders also are less likely than men to be employed, have lower household income, and a significantly lower median portfolio value ($4,100) than men ($7,400). It appears there is still considerable progress to be made in encouraging women to become more knowledgeable and, therefore, active participants in the equity markets. Passively waiting to acquire stocks through gift or inheritance is not likely to produce a sub-stantial-enough portfolio to fund the special financial risks women will face. All in all, upon closer inspection, the data seems to support results reported elsewhere that women are less likely than men to invest actively in the market.

7. Demystifying Interest

In 1975, the Census Bureau reported that more women received income from a job than from any other source. But by 1982, a startling shift had occurred. By 1982, for the first time, more women reported receiving income from interest than from any other source. In that year, 49,763,000 women (53.5 percent of all women) reported receiving some amount of interest income, compared to 49,481,000 women (53.1 percent) who reported receiving at least some income from a job. And though these numbers do not reflect the dollar value of the income source—while 53 percent of all women receive some income from interest, interest income did not (and does not) account for most of our earnings—what the numbers do show is that we women have a great stake in learning to understand, and therefore to better manage, interest.

Because interest plays so pervasive a role in our financial lives, it is almost assumed that everyone knows the basics of interest. But interest can be intimidating. Many of us are embarrassed by what we do not know about interest. Interest, like certain algebra problems from eighth grade, is one of those things we believe we should have learned a long time ago, so long ago that many of us are ashamed to admit as adults that we really do not understand it. Some of us may have faked understanding back in eighth grade when all the other kids seemed to know the answer. But the shame of it is, even many of those kids who seemed to know the answer probably also were lost. The consequence is that a lot of people buy cars without knowing how to calculate the annual percentage rate (APR). Some buy without knowing what the acronym APR means. A lot of people sign thirty-year adjustable rate mortgages for hundreds of thousand of dollars—in many cases the single biggest financial deal of their lives—without knowing how to calculate the mortgage interest rate. And a lot of people invest their life savings without really understanding the difference between simple and compound interest.

Recently, I read about a man named John Corcoran. John is an intelligent man who had achieved great success as a father, husband, and businessman. In his career, John had held down challenging jobs, including a stint as a teacher. But John had a secret. He had hidden this secret from his wife, from his fellow teachers, and later in life when he became a successful developer, from his employees. His secret? John could not read.

Being naturally quick, John had developed ways of compensating for his inability to read and had been so clever at hiding the truth that no one, not even fellow teachers, had suspected. For example, he avoided writing on the blackboard and, when he had to, he made sure he copied perfectly what someone else had written. And when he left teaching to run his own business, he found it was easy merely to order subordinates to read contracts or other material. Still, he confessed, without an ability to figure out words, he had to rely on others for clues. In other words, he had to trust. He had no other choice.

If trusting subordinates to read contracts sounds dangerous, it is no more dangerous than trusting others to tell you what interest rate you should be paying (or receiving). This is not trust. It is an invitation for mishap. "Thirty to thirty-five percent of the monthly charges on the 12 million outstanding adjustable-rate mortgages contain billing errors," according to John Geddes, a former federal mortgage banking auditor and whistleblower. He estimates that half of all homeowners are charged too much, with the net overcharges amounting to almost $8 billion. The Government Accounting Office's official estimate is that as many as one out of every four homeowners with adjustable rate mortgages may be overcharged (or undercharged) each month because of bank calculation errors. These mistakes can result in the total overpayment of thousands of dollars in mortgage interest each year. A Florida couple, Shirley and Gordon Wynn of Miami, recently received a refund of $1,463.99 from Coral Gables Federal Savings and Loan because of the bank's erroneous overcharge of interest on their adjustable rate mortgage. After being corrected, their monthly mortgage payment dropped from $812.34 to $797.75. Are you being overcharged for interest on your mortgage? On your car? Is your pension plan undercrediting your account? Unless you understand interest, you have no choice but to trust.

APRs, mortgage interest rates, compound interest, rates of return, yield—these all are concepts which can be mastered once you break down the concept of interest. Once and for all, let's try to clear things up.

Interest Is Rent

Money, like real estate or any other asset, has rental value. When you use other people's money, as, for example, when you borrow from a bank to buy a house or car, you are renting their money. Interest is the rent charged for the use of such money.

Interest may be simple or compound. Simple interest is the amount of rent charged for the use of money, without the reinvestment of interest. For example, you invest $100 at 5 percent per year. At the end of the year, you receive $105. At the end of two years, you receive another $5, bringing the total amount of interest received over the two-year period to $10.

The equation for interest is a basic rule of money's flow. In the example above, at the end of year one, you received $105. That $105 represents the accumulated value of $100 at 5 percent simple interest for a one-year period. And $110 represents the accumulated value of $100 at 5 percent simple interest for a two-year period.

To generalize, if "A" stands for accumulated value, "I" for the amount you invest, "i" for the interest rate, and "t" for the time period over which the investment grows, then

$$A = I[1 + i(t)]$$

In our example for a 1-year period, the equation to determine accumulated value is

$$A = \$100\ [1 + .05\ (1\ year)]$$

$$= \$100 + 100\ (.05)$$

$$= \$100 + 5$$

$$= \$105.$$

And for a 2-year period, the accumulated value would be

$$A = \$100\ [1 + .05(2)]$$

$$= \$100\ [1 + .10]$$

$$= \$100\ [1.10]$$

$$= \$110.$$

The calculation of accumulated value of money invested at a simple interest rate probably seems intuitive. You basically are multiplying interest by time period by the amount invested.

Compound interest is the rent charged for the use of money with reinvestment of interest. Thus, compound interest enables the payment of interest on interest.

To use our example, over a one-year period, if interest is paid once a year, $100 invested at 5 percent compound interest will accumulate to $105. After two years, the advantage of compound interest begins to appear. The $5 you earn at the end of the first year is reinvested with your initial

$100 at a 5 percent rate, producing ($105)(1.05) = $110.25. The extra $.25 represents the return of interest on interest.

Again, to generalize, if "A" is the accumulated value, "I" is the amount of your initial investment, "i" for the interest rate and "t" for the time period over which the investment grows, then

$$A = I(1 + i)^t$$

This is an exponential equation. If, for example, t = 2 years, the amount within the parentheses should be squared. If t = 3, the sum within the parentheses should be cubed; if t = 4, the sum should be quadrupled and so on. As you can see, compounding interest can produce extraordinary growth over longer periods.

So, how much money would you have if you invested $100 at 5 percent compound interest rate for two years?

$$A = \$100 (1 + .05)^2$$

$$= \$100 (1.05)^2$$

$$= \$100 (1.1025)$$

$$= \$110.25$$

How much would you have if you invested $100 at 8 percent compound interest for ten years? The result would be:

$$A = \$100 (1 + .08) \text{ to the tenth power}$$

$$= \$100 (2.1589)$$

$$= \$215.89$$

So your money more than doubles at 8 percent compound interest in ten years.

Multiplying a number to the tenth power, while it can be done manually, is easy with a calculator. You should consider investing in one with an exponential function, unless you are extraordinarily patient at multiplying numbers.

The number of times compound interest is reinvested will affect the accumulated value. The more frequently interest is compounded, the higher the accumulated value.

The formula for compound interest reinvested at a frequency other than yearly is

   A = I (1 + i/N) raised to the Nt power

This formula may look intimidating—don't give up now, we're almost done!—but it is actually straightforward. If interest is compounded quarterly, N=4, for example. If interest is compounded semiannually, N=2. If interest is compounded each day of the year, N=365.

To use an example, let's find the accumulated value after two years of $100 invested at 5 percent interest compounded quarterly. Recall that the answer for interest compounded once a year is $110.25. If the interest is compounded quarterly, the formula would produce:

   A = $100(1 +.05/4) raised to the 4x2 power, since N=4
       and t=2

     = $100(1 + .0125) raised to the 8th power

     = $100(1.1044)

     = $110.45

Thus, you get an extra $.45 rather than $.25, almost double the amount of compounded interest when the frequency is quarterly rather than annually. And while this difference may not seem dazzling for a relatively small sum, these differences add up as the amounts involved increase and the time periods lengthen.

Financial institutions may compound interest at different frequencies. At most larger commercial banks in New York, for example, interest on savings is compounded daily, though it is paid only monthly.

Rate of Return and Yield

As you have seen, interest can be thought of as "rent" on money. It can also be thought of as the profit earned on money. Both ways of viewing interest try to represent the compensation earned for allowing use of money.

If, for example, you put $1,000 in a savings account and the bank pays 5 percent on all savings accounts, the interest rate is 5 percent. The bank pays 5 percent regardless of the amount you deposit, whether it be $100 or $10,000.

By contrast, *rate of return* and *yield* are concepts expressing the amount of profit earned relative to the purchase price of the investment product.

If for each dollar invested you earn a nickel, the rate of return is 5 percent. If, for example, you buy a bond for $1,000 paying $100 a year, the interest rate—called a coupon rate—is 10 percent. If the same bond trades down to $800, the interest rate remains 10 percent, but the yield increases to 100/800, or 12.5 percent.

Rates of return and yields, like other forms of interest compensation, make no sense in a time vacuum. They must be expressed relative to a given period, usually one year.

When comparing rates of return and yields, make sure you are comparing apples to apples. Returns or yields expressed in other than annual terms should be "annualized." For example, a six-month certificate of deposit paying 4.75 percent would be annualized to a rate of 9.5 percent.

Usury

Most states have usury laws limiting the amount of interest that may be charged for the use of money. Because most usury laws were enacted to protect presumably unsophisticated non-business consumers, usury laws often except from their application corporate or other business borrowers. The rationale here is that business entities can fend for themselves.

Why do major banks located in states such as New York or California run their credit card operations out of places like Sioux Falls, South Dakota? The answer to the mystery lies in differing usury rates. South Dakota has one of the highest usury limits in the nation, allowing a financial institution to charge up to 19.8 percent on credit cards.

So, it pays to compare credit card rates. Be especially wary if your local bank has credit operations out of state for no apparent reason. It could signal that a much better rate is available if you shop around.

Finally, as a general matter, you should review (or better yet have your attorney review) major loan agreements for usury waiver clauses. These clauses basically try to have you waive your defense of usury if the rate exceeds the state's usury limits. Some states, fearing that the effect of these waiver clauses would be to circumvent the usury protections, make it legally impossible for you to waive your usury defense.

8. Seven Financial Habits That Can Change Your Life

You have seen, in Parts One and Two of this book, the special financial risks women face throughout our lives. You have seen how a woman's failure to manage these risks can all but determine her financial fate. You have also, hopefully, seen tools to help you begin to reorder your financial house: identifying when you are over-giving, learning to resign as family banker, setting up a relatively painless way to save monthly with self-bills and automatic account builders, sorting out financial roles with your spouse, and identifying what investment risks you should take for the reward promised. What the explorations have shown, thus far, can be summarized as seven investment habits, habits which, if followed, could change your financial future. To change your financial future for the better, you must learn to:

1. Put Yourself First.

Women, socialized as caretakers, learn early on that we are valued in society for being resources for others. And we become experts at being assets to others. We learn to look after others in almost every facet of our lives, at home, on the job, with our friends. But what we are not taught, and therefore what many of us never learn, is how to be good to ourselves. How to take care of, look after, and value ourselves. It is not surprising that we also do not learn to look after and value our financial selves. We tend to take care of all else and all others before we reach our own needs. But this priority is not writ large across the heavens. Nowhere is it written that we cannot change that habit of putting ourselves last. We can learn—we must learn—that putting ourselves first is not bad. It is not a denial of ourselves as women. It does not make us bad mothers or bad wives or bad daughters or bad friends. It only makes us self-possessed.

I have known, met, interviewed, and read about many exceptional women, but I can probably count on one hand those women who truly put themselves first, value themselves, without feeling they somehow have subtracted from their commitments to motherhood, daughterhood, and wifehood. How do these few do it? Well, they have somehow learned along the way that it pays to treat yourself well in all respects. It only makes good sense to do so, since you spend more time with yourself than with any other human. Over an eighty-year lifetime, a woman spends 29,200 days with herself—29,200! Yet how many of those days are devoted to figuring out how to treat herself better? A handful? How many have you spent?

What if, starting today, you spent five minutes each day planning to better your financial health? Imagine, you could spend those five minutes:

- forming a plan for the next year

- making a checklist of the things you can do daily, weekly, or monthly to improve your earnings or your savings

- evaluating how you are losing money and discovering ways to plug cash drains in your life

- recommitting yourself to goal-setting and goal-achievement

Isn't the achievement of goals so significant to your over-all well-being worth five minutes a day?

Earlier we quoted psychologist William Kaufman's obser-vation that people throughout their lives are more or less continuously concerned with the solution of their private money problems. But what we also have seen is that, though most people may be continuously concerned, they are not spending this time being concerned in a productive way. Instead, they are wasting time worrying when they should be spending time planning and acting on a plan. Choose a regular time during the day, maybe your lunch hour, maybe on the way home, and set aside these five minutes to sort out where you have been, where you are, and, most importantly, where you are going financially.

2. Separate Long-Term Planning from Short.

Most of us make a critical error in setting goals and eval-uating financial options: We do not separate long-term from short-term goals or investment products suitable for long-term planning from those suitable for the short term. Here is what I mean. If you focus only on the long term, what you may produce as a list of goals are funding retirement, college costs for kids, providing for eldercare, and so on. As we have seen, products suitable for meeting these goals should feature capital appreciation, such as common stocks, growth mutual funds, and real estate. These prod-ucts, especially stocks, may have bad short-term perfor-mance. Over a one-year or even five-year period, the return on invested capital may indeed appear dismally inadequate. Fearing the volatility of the sometimes rollercoaster-like swings in stocks, many women give up on them. They eliminate stocks from all but an insubstantial part of their total investment picture. As a result, they lose out on their best chance for meeting their long-term needs. They are asking long-term products to meet short-term expectations of gain. It just won't work.

The best approach to take is to begin a monthly program of investing a fixed amount in stocks and mutuals as part of a long-term program to fund your long-term needs. Then, and this is the important habit to acquire, leave it alone. Let the gains accumulate without checking daily on their progress. Let it happen. To summarize, once you have set in place a long-term investment program, let it happen automatically. Do not trouble a long-term program with short-term worries.

3. Resign as Family Banker.

The socialization of women as caretakers sometimes is too thorough for our own good. And when it comes to lending a helping hand, many of us are compulsive. We do not know how to stop giving until we have given all too much. But you were not born a family banker. It is not a job description written on your birth certificate. You are entitled to say when enough is enough. However, it is up to you to say when. Use your voice. Those who borrow without regard to your personal needs will not stop asking until you start demonstrating when you have had enough. Send different signals. When they complain about how hard it is to make ends meet, counter-complain about how tough it is for you to make ends meet. When they refuse to pay you back or to use the money they have borrowed as agreed, remind them of it. Keep a list of the loans they have not paid back, dates, amounts, etc. Carry a copy of this list with you so that when you are "ambushed" with loan requests, you can rid yourself of guilt by reminding yourself that you already have given enough.

4. Leave Home Without It: Don't Carry Money.

It is human nature that things put in front of our faces will command our attention, be used more, thought of more. If you have money in your hands, in your purse, the fact of the matter is that you are more likely to use it. So leave it at home. Only carry what you need to make it through the day. Leave checkbooks at home. If you need to pay a bill while you are out during the day, make out the check before you leave home and leave the rest of the checkbook behind. And, contrary to a popular credit card commercial, *you should leave home without it*. Taking it with you invites you to indulge in one of the most damaging financial habits—impulse spending. Do not carry extra cash. Do not carry spare plastic. Do not carry around extra purchasing power. You will use it.

5. Haggle.

Women, as we have seen, pay significantly more than men for goods with negotiable prices. Car dealers and sellers of homes are probably not the only ones who give women worse deals than men in part because women fail to haggle. A good rule of thumb to remember is to cut in half your estimate of the seller's bottom line. This will help you to correct for what appears to be a reluctance among many women to drive a seller closer to his or her bottom line. Whether buying homes, negotiating salary raises or severance pay, or selling goods and services yourself, developing the habit of haggling can save you hundreds of thousands of dollars over the course of your life.

6. Don't Put Your Money Anywhere Your Brain's Not Welcome.

Whenever you invest your money or your credit, whether in stocks, in your spouse's business, or in your business, always be skeptical of endeavors where you have no say. Be skeptical of investments with disclosure documents that are not written plainly. Be skeptical of opportunities where someone has assured you that he or she will "take care of the details." For every investment is a story, a story that is trying to sell itself. And to consistently invest well, you have to know how to read that story. You have to know how to analyze that story's flaws. Be especially wary of lending your name as a guarantor or co-lender on loans where you have no input into how the business is run. It does not matter that the enterprise is your husband's business and that he says, "Honey, you'll benefit when I'll benefit." If you are not in voice when decisions are made that determine whether the enterprise can pay off the loan, you are investing blindly.

7. Keep Enough Mad Money to Get You Back Home.

The mad money your mom pinned to your blouse to get you back home no matter how badly things fell apart is still a great idea. Women, especially, need to save for those crazy circumstances when your ally-spouse turns enemy or when you lose your job or when life for any number of reasons goes mad. When you cannot count on rationality, count on yourself and your mad money account. Mad dollars can be the best dollars of all. Mad dollars are smart dollars. They are the angry dollars that survive the disillusionment of divorce. They are the savvy dollars that stay tucked away in stock accounts, safe from spending splurges. They are the wise dollars that help you thrive in retirement.

Many of us go through life with a Pollyana-ish belief that it will all work out somehow. But, to paraphrase Rabbi Harold Kushner, bad things can and do often happen to good women. Yes, your mother may need nursing home care and your siblings may not help out as much as they should; yes, you may never get that promotion you deserve; yes, the marriage may break up. To turn the odds in your favor, you must plan and plan and plan some more. Mad money should represent savings above and beyond your normal savings plan. You should be extremely protective of your mad money. It should not be used for your cousin's rainy day or your spouse's rainy day. Your mad money is for *your* rainy day.

How do you accumulate mad money on top of all your other savings goals? You do it by shaving pennies. How much do you spend on coffee or cigarettes per day? Per week? Start shaving pennies from these kinds of luxuries for that day when no one will come to your rescue but you.

You may have heard the parable of the effect of making small changes in your life. Two ships set across the ocean from the same port, traveling at the same speed, following the same course. But shortly after embarking, the first ship veers slightly, a change of only a few degrees. No one is concerned, so no one changes course. Besides, after the first two miles, passengers on the two ships are still close enough to see each other waving. But, as the journey lengthens, the small change of degree in the courses of the ships begins to make a difference, and after two hours the distance between the ships has grown so much that, though they can still make out a ship in the distance, the passengers can no longer see each other waving. Soon, the ships are no longer visible to each other. When they finally reach land again, one ship is in Europe and the other in Australia. Small degrees of difference, applied over large distances, produce vastly different outcomes. Likewise, small degrees of difference in your daily financial habits, applied over the course of a lifetime, can dramatically alter your ultimate financial destination.

Acquire these seven habits. Begin to make a change.

Creating an Investment Plan

Creating an investment plan involves two jobs. The first job is to identify goals. The second is to match goals with suitable investment products. To identify investment goals, we explored the special financial needs of women: funding retirement, saving mad money in case of divorce or separation, funding childcare and eldercare, saving for college, etc. And if you have completed the form in Appendix A, you have assessed your current allocation of assets, an assessment that might have revealed that your current asset allocation does not adequately address the special risks you face. Finally, we discussed some of the emotional battles you may have to settle en route to clarifying money's role in your life and reaching a better-tailored asset allocation, explored the tradeoff between investment risk and return, and, we hope, made you more assertive and comfortable in figuring out how much interest you should be paid on your interest-bearing assets or how much you should be paying on your mortgage and other obligations. In sum, figuring out your investment goals in light of the special risks women face has been the concern of Parts One and Two.

Figuring out in greater detail the risk and return characteristics of various investment products is the concern of

Part Three. Because of the importance of this inquiry, we devote the next four chapters to individual exploration of the basic categories of assets available for investment. In the order in which they will be discussed, the basic four investment choices are cash, real estate, securities, and insurance.

part three:

THE BASIC FOUR INVESTMENT CHOICES

9. Cash and Near-Cash

Just How Safe Is Cash?

As historically risk-averse investors, women flock to ports of safety. As we have seen, we women keep far more of our dollars in banks than men. And the rationale repeated often is "to keep them safe" or, as one woman put it, "out of harm's way." Every mother already knows a lot about keeping assets out of harm's way.

To keep our most precious assets, our children, safe and out of harm's way, we would do almost anything. We tuck the blanket under their chins, kiss them goodnight, and say silent prayers for their safety. But even as we close the door, we know that keeping them close at home forever is not always the best way to ensure their safety. And as we become more experienced as parents, we learn to hold our breath and let them venture into the world, to learn, play, fall down, take risks, and, in doing so, to grow. For children shut in all their lives cannot hope to cope successfully against real-world risks. In what seems like a paradox, we must let them experience some forms of risks to prepare them to face far greater ones.

In a way, we face a similar choice when it comes to deciding whether to keep all our assets in cash in banks. With banks, there is a perception of safety from the vicissitudes of markets, what one woman, Elaine, who works for a Wall Street investment house, calls, "the wackiness of Wall

Street." And the metaphor for decades for the cinch, the no-fail, has been, "It's like money in the bank."

But the long-held belief that nothing is safer than money in the bank has been razed by the bulldozer of the S&L scandal and the growing troubles of the banking industry. Now, you can find lines of worried depositors, their faces a frozen, confused rictus, clenching their bank statements and wondering whether they will need those thrown-away bank deposit slips as proof.

Many, like some in the line to receive their deposits from the failed Freedom National Bank in New York, are angry. They feel betrayed. "Why didn't they let us know they were in trouble," one elderly woman complains. "I was in there on Thursday, and you never would have thought anything was up. The tellers were smiling. You never know."

The S&L scandal and the bank failures have underlined once again a financial truth we should never forget. Every investment form, including cash, has inherent risks. Some inherent risks are less obvious than others. In this section, we explore what these risks are and the appropriate allocation of cash and products with nearly the same risks as cash, so-called near-cash.

Payment Risk

Prior to the savings and loan fiasco and the growing number of bank failures, federal insurance was believed by some to extend to each account a person had at an institution, regardless of the number of accounts held there. Many mistakenly believed that federal insurance covers all accounts at an institution up to $100,000. And many people relying on this common misconception were left holding the bag.

As a general matter, the rule is that the government insures only up to $100,000 per person at an institution. Thus, the simplest way to keep your money safe is never to have more than $100,000 in a single institution. However, many people are unaware that buried deep in arcane federal statutory language are two particularly useful exceptions to the general rule. One, there is an exception for accounts held in other capacities, such as in an IRA or a Keogh plan. Two, there is an exception for money held in joint accounts. Under this exception, the government insures your share of money held jointly, such as in joint accounts with your husband or children, up to a maximum of $100,000.

For example, a woman who has $100,000 in a bank in one or more individual accounts and $100,000 in an IRA would have the full $200,000 covered. If she also had several joint accounts, say, $80,000 in a joint account with her husband, $40,000 in a joint account with her son and $40,000 in a joint account with her daughter, she would have an additional $80,000 insured, representing 50 percent of the total of her joint accounts. As you can see, it is possible to stretch government insurance above $100,000 if you know and use the rules.

At any rate, if you have significant amounts of money over $100,000 in a bank or savings and loan, you owe it to yourself to make sure you qualify for one of the exceptions to the one-account-per-institution rule. Call the FDIC directly. Do not rely merely on what the bank or S&L tells you, as even some government officials warn. "I would suggest that in complicated situations people not take the institution's word for it that all accounts are insured," recommends David M. Barr, a Federal Deposit Insurance Corporation (FDIC) spokesman. "A common thread at many failed banks and savings institutions is that they said accounts were insured when in fact they were not."

Near-cash assets are like cash in that they are relatively liquid and present little or no payment risk. Government obligations, such as Treasury bills, Treasury notes and Treasury bonds, fall into this category. We say they are near-cash because they are not entirely free of payment risk. However, because these products carry the "full faith and credit" guarantee of the United States, the market considers them risk-free. That is, the government guarantees investors the principal and interest due them. But even these investments are not "safe" from the effects of inflation. For example, if inflation is running at a rate of 5 percent, a Treasury bill, or T-bill, bearing an 8 percent rate of return is really returning only 3 percent interest. To use another example, a T-bill returning 5 percent in a 6 percent inflationary environment actually has a negative 1 percent return. In fact, long-term studies of the returns of Treasury bills have shown these returns have a tendency to track inflation with the result that the real, inflation-adjusted returns are close to zero. And, you may be surprised to learn, for significant stretches of time, the net returns on these products have in fact been negative.

Another risk for interest-bearing cash and near-cash investments is the application of tax laws. Here, unless the investment is eligible for tax-free treatment under the Internal Revenue Code, you will have to pay taxes on the investment, thereby reducing your net profit. The tax cut can be deep. In the case of an investor in the 28 percent bracket holding a 5 percent T-bill, the real tax-adjusted return is only 3.5 percent. Adjusted both for taxes and inflation, the return can be negative. So, as you can see, even keeping your money entirely in the so-called "safest" investments can, in the long run, be a losing strategy. Because of the erosive effects of inflation and taxes, doing nothing is not tantamount to treading water. It may mean you are slowly drowning.

More on Inflation

Cash investments inherently are at risk for losing value because of the effect of inflation. As inflation increases, the purchasing power, and, therefore, the value of cash decreases. A cash portfolio of $100,000, in an inflationary environment of 5 percent annually, will be worth only $95,000 in purchasing power by year's end. In fact, at an annual inflation rate of only 4 percent, money loses half its value in 18 years.

You often hear news reports on "the rate of inflation," and, like most people, you begin to worry. If inflation rises 5 percent, you become immediately concerned whether your salary will keep up with inflation. As reported, inflation seems almost a monolithic concept. But actually, inflation is a piecemeal, spotty concept.

To see why this is so, you have to examine how the government derives the rate of inflation. The rate of inflation is based on a measure of the prices of a set bundle of goods and services. The government has selected the particular goods and services placed inside the all-important measuring bundle. Thus, if the price of the items in the bundle is 5 percent more than the price of the same bundle a year before, the "rate of inflation" is reported as 5 percent. But the goods you actually purchase each year in all likelihood do not match the government's bundle exactly. While the government may have avocadoes and Chevrolets in its bundle, you may have mangoes and Toyotas in yours. As a result, your personal "rate of inflation" may be higher or lower than the government's rate of inflation. That is, since each individual consumer has a different bundle, the government's rate of inflation is not a universally useful, or more precisely, a universally applicable figure. The rate that really counts is your *personal inflation rate.*

What role should cash play in your investment portfolio? Because cash has no payment risk, it should represent the bulk of the reserves you would use in an emergency. A sound asset allocation would keep at least six-months' living expenses in cash. Another six-months of living expenses should be kept in near-cash. Of this amount, five months should be kept in interest-earning products, such as money market accounts, and no more than one month in non-interest bearing forms, such as certain checking accounts.

10. Real Estate

Real estate, as an investment, has had a storied career. Though it is difficult for some post-World War II Americans to believe, real estate was not always sold on television like detergent. The American dream, as it pertained to real estate, was to own a home, not to own a mega-empire of rental properties worth millions. Certain financial advisers believe in Real-Estate-as-Gold. Like modern P.T. Barnums, they draw crowds with fantastic claims of what is behind the tent. "Walk with me," they say, and "I'll show you how to buy the American dream." Better yet, "I'll show you how to buy America for no money down!"

Now, there is usually some truth in these fantasies. Usually, in fact, there is just enough truth to make them believable. For example, there are properties in some neighborhoods, in some cities, during some periods, that can be bought for no money down and that will produce a tidy profit. But there are other situations where the no-money-down strategy is a prescription for financial disaster. This is especially true for those converts who do not have enough cash reserves to ride out the rough spots in the market. In these cases, the buyer of a property with no money down may find the cost of paying the mortgage on the 100 percent-financed property is higher than the cash flow the property produces. She may find the monthly negative cash flow too much to handle. Moreover, the scenarios where no money down works may depend on maintaining a fragile equilibrium among property values (it must be an appreciating market), rental income (it must be high enough to cover the mortgage), and mortgage interest rates (they should be stable or falling, not rising). If any of these factors falls out of line, the negative cash flow can drown you.

To invest consistently well in real estate, you must identify the basis on which you are buying the property. Are you buying the property because of its potential to appreciate in value? Or are you mainly interested in its cash-flow stream? Or its tax advantages? All these reasons? Having determined your objectives, you then must identify and challenge the assumptions underlying the seller's picture of the property. That is, you must challenge assumptions underlying cash-flow projections, valuations, tax deductibility, and so on.

Let's assume you are buying a property for its potential to appreciate in value and its tax benefits. One key assumption usually made is that the general trend of real estate values for the location under consideration is upward. In fact, for most of post-World War II America, this assumption was correct. One of the surest bets you could make was to invest in a house, live there for five or ten years, and sell at a nice profit.

But as the late 1980s and early 1990s have taught us, even a sure thing is not always so sure. And, real estate's once untarnished image as a wealth builder has taken a severe beating. Even Manhattan real estate, once considered the most coveted real estate in the world, has fallen victim to the auctioneer's gavel. As developer after developer files public documents revealing their deteriorating financial condition, the cachet of invincibility that once surrounded the real estate market has evaporated. In its place a new sobriety about the profitability of real estate has emerged. Now, some respected academics have urged us to discard our belief that the arrow indicating the general trend for real estate invariably points up. They predict that the general trend for real estate even for the next several decades will be downward.

Not all who invest in real estate will do badly, even in soft markets. Some of you will have analyzed successfully the underlying assumptions of your purchases. A far rarer few who might have made analytic or management mistakes will be tided over during soft markets by banks willing to restructure their debt. Banks are willing to help you restructure your debt if the restructuring either helps them to make more money or to lose less money than they would if they let you sink. This equation produces apparently strange results. Some banks will, for example, painstakingly restructure a multi-billion-dollar loan but will foreclose in less than a heartbeat on small homeowners. Banks faced with the prospect of foreclosing on large properties may face a loss of hundreds of millions of dollars. So in this situation, the smarter move for them may very well be to finance the billion-dollar restructuring, wait until the market stabilizes, then sell the assets in a more orderly way. In this way, they avoid selling at firesale prices. So while it may seem illogical or downright unfair to some that the more debt you owe, the more likely a bank is to bail you out, the decision often is motivated by the common-sense desire to minimize losses and maximize profits.

The same logic can work on a smaller scale if the small loan is not too costly to administer during the workout. Unfortunately, however, when it comes to small homeowners, banks are much less apt to recognize the potential mutual advantages of restructuring. And the too-big-to-fail safety net, which catches many a millionaire before the fall, has holes more than large enough for most struggling homeowners to slip through. You are not too big to fail. To succeed in real estate, you must do some homework.

What's This House Worth?

If you are buying property on the basis of its potential to appreciate, your homework should include, at a minimum, an analysis of the:

1. Values of the surrounding properties

2. Vitality of the local economy

3. Demographics of the potential rental market.

The first factor, the values of surrounding properties, should be measured by recent actual sales. Remember, what you are trying to figure out is the answer to the age-old question, "What's this property worth?" You should avoid relying on offers that your seller or neighboring sellers quote. You should also be wary of relying on quotes supplied by real estate agents, who, because they receive a higher commission for a larger sales price, have an incentive to quote the highest price you are willing to pay. And even though the agent may tell you in a conspiratorial whisper that, "That's only the asking price, the seller's really willing to take $X," the $X is probably still higher than the rock bottom price.

The vitality of the city and state in which the property is located also critically affects the potential for appreciation. The law of supply and demand controls. So, as a general rule, if the local economy is thriving and incomes are rising, more people will need housing, and they will bid up housing values. And if housing prices are bid up at a faster rate than the rate of inflation, you will net a profit upon resale. But if the local economy is sluggish, incomes are stable or falling, and there is no pressure to bid up housing prices, housing values may fall, as they have in certain areas of the country during the early 1990s.

Moreover, when it comes to housing, what you may discover is that certain cities have local inflation rates slower or faster than the state or national rate. The housing values in your location may outstrip the national inflation rate but lag behind the local inflation rate. Thus, you may find that even though upon resale your house has appreciated 20 percent and the national inflation rate over the same period has been 10 percent, because your local inflation rate is 21 percent (and you buy your goods locally after all), you really have not netted a profit. One observation that should temper your concern about divergent inflation rates is that, as a general rule, over the long term, the national and local rates of inflation have tended to converge because of interstate commerce.

The third factor you should consider if you are buying property based on the potential for appreciation is the demographics of the area. Is this a college town, where you are likely to have a steady supply of students needing rental housing? Is the city growing in population? Are young families moving in, or is this the kind of town people cannot wait to leave after they reach adulthood? The data you need here is the age and income profile of the population likely to rent your property.

Most of these factors are derived by common sense. There is no exact science to predicting which properties will do well. But the factors identified above should help you greatly in weeding out those properties that are unlikely to appreciate. Once you have eliminated the clear clunkers, you have reduced the downside risk to a reasonable level. And while you may not experience spectacular growth in your portfolio, you will have greatly increased your chances of seeing at least moderate appreciation.

What is a house worth? The answer really depends on whom you ask. So far, we have answered the question from the perspective of you as a potential purchaser of the home. Others have different views of the house. You will find at least five different perspectives of what any house is worth. How those perspectives differ is perhaps best shown in the drawing on the next page by an unknown artist.

Tax Considerations

Finally, you may buy property solely because of the tax advantages. Under the current version of the Internal Revenue Code, property holders can deduct all mortgage interest payments. This is true regardless of whether you use the house as your principal residence, your second home, or as an investment rental property. But in addition to mortgage interest rates, you incur other expenses in owning real estate, such as insurance premiums, state and local taxes, and maintenance and repair costs. Of these costs, only some are deductible, and the percentage of deductibility depends on the type of property and the purpose for which the property is used. For example, state and local taxes are fully deductible for properties used as primary residences, so long as the property itself is owned 100

The Unreliable Eye

Your HOUSE as seen by...

...yourself

...the builder

...your bank

...your fire-insurance company

...the tax assessor

percent by the taxpayer. In property law, such outright ownership of all rights in the property is called a "fee simple." Examples of fee simple ownership that would entitle you to 100 percent deductibility of state and local taxes include single family detached houses, townhouses, and condominiums.

Unlike single family detached houses or condominiums, cooperatives are not owned by individuals in fee simple. Cooperatives are corporations that own property. The corporation takes out the mortgage on the entire property and pays all taxes, maintenance costs, and so on. The individual "homeowner" in a cooperative really owns only shares in the corporation. She no more owns the bricks, floors, and ceilings of her home than a shareholder of IBM owns its computers.

After the cooperative-corporation determines how much taxes as a whole it owes the state and city, it then assesses each individual cooperative shareholder's fees in proportion to the number of shares she owns in the cooperative. If she owns 50 percent of the cooperative, she pays 50 percent of the tax bill. If she owns .8 percent of the cooperative, she pays .8 percent of the tax bill. Surprisingly, some co-op owners actually neglect to deduct their share of taxes paid.

If the property is a condominium or cooperative, the amount of state and city taxes you pay depends on the tax agreement between the taxing authority and the developer of the property. Some developers in New York, for example, bargain ferociously to acquire tax abatements for ten years or more. Why states agree to grant developers these tax abatements, and why some developers get them and others do not, is a subject of much head-scratching in political quarters, but suffice it to say, these abatements are granted to promote the building of properties. If you live in a building with a tax abatement, your taxes will be reduced for the period of the abatement. It therefore pays to investigate not only whether the building you're considering investing in has such an abatement but, equally as important, how many years are left before the abatement runs out.

Certain properties are not assessed any taxes at all. Some states have acquired property in the state's name and as a matter of law do not assess taxes on such properties. For example, the State of New York owns Roosevelt Island, which sits in the middle of the East River between Manhattan and Queens. Most of the island faces the Upper East Side of Manhattan and has access to Manhattan by subway and a tram. The Roosevelt Island Development Corporation, a not-for-profit corporation set up by the State of New York, plans to have a major site on the island developed as cooperative or condominium residences. Since the state will not assess taxes on the development, homeowners will pay no taxes. The only fees in this regard will be certain small payments-in-lieu-of-taxes, PILOTs, which are minuscule compared with a normal tax assessment.

Unlike taxes, insurance, maintenance, and repair costs ordinarily are not tax deductible. Some homeowners, however, convert these costs into tax deductible costs by using their homes to run businesses, since expenses incurred in a business or trade are fully deductible. But what does the IRS consider a "business or trade"? It may surprise you to learn that neither the Internal Revenue Code nor IRS regulations define what is meant by a trade or business. The closest the agency comes is in IRS Publication 334, "Tax Guide for Small Business," in which a trade or business is defined as:

1. An activity carried on for livelihood or for profit.

2. An activity in which a profit motive is present and where there is some type of economic activity involved. As to the profit motive, an activity will be considered a business if it is entered into and carried on in good faith for the purpose of making a profit, *as opposed to an activity engaged in purely for self-satisfaction.*

3. An enterprise that is characterized by regularity of activities and transactions and the production of income. The absence of income, in itself, will not prevent an enter-

prise from being classified as a trade or business but could raise a question as to whether a business was carried on in a particular year. In such a case a taxpayer should be able to show that he or she actually was in business during that year.

As you can see, the IRS' view of what constitutes a business depends on some rather vague notions. When is an activity "engaged in purely for self-satisfaction" so as not to qualify as a business? Perhaps taxpayers ought to make sure that even if we are engaged in supporting our families, we take care not to enjoy it too much lest we lose our tax deductions.

Taxpayers who have incurred expenses in renting property have much more success in deducting these costs. Under Internal Revenue Code Section 212, certain expenses can be deducted as having been incurred "in the production or collection of income." However, the IRS has disallowed these deductions where it was shown that the taxpayer was not using the property to obtain rental income but instead was using the property to benefit family members. For example, a taxpayer who rented residential property to a son-in-law and other family members for an excessively low rent was not allowed to deduct rental expenses.

Be wary in dealing with IRS deductions. The IRS uses tremendous discretion in labeling activities as businesses or not. And what you thought was your business may be classified as your hobby. The best—but by no means fail-safe—approach is to find and use competent tax counsel before you venture too far into the murky waters of IRS definitions.

Mortgages

Deciding how to finance a property affects its profitability as much as the selection of the property itself. Mortgages historically have represented the largest single financing in an individual's life. And though most consumers know the basic differences among mortgages available, certain common mortgage features that can greatly reduce mortgage costs are overlooked.

The lender, technically the "mortgagee," extends credit to the "mortgagor," and takes as security for the loan a lien, the "mortgage." Mortgages may be classified according to whether they (1) are first, second, third or even more subordinated liens, (2) are conventional or government-insured, (3) allow prepayments of principal (4) are fixed-rate or have one or more versions of an adjustable interest rate or variable payment schedule and (5) the term of the mortgage. Mortgages also differ according to the types of notification and work-out rights you are entitled to if you miss payments. And, as has been well-publicized, lenders differ with respect to the amount of mortgage they are willing to extend for a given property and the closing fees you must incur. These fees typically are expressed as a percentage of the mortgage with one percent of the mortgage equalling a "point."

Adjustable rate mortgages were created as a way to let financial institutions match the liabilities they paid as interest on the savings accounts of their customers to the assets they held in the form of mortgages. When mortgages had fixed rates only, savings and loan institutions were especially hard pressed to match liabilities and assets. This occurred because the funds the banks and thrifts used to make the mortgages came from the savings accounts of their customers. The rates the banks and thrifts paid to the customers on pass-book savings accounts represent a cost on their financial statements, known aptly enough as the "cost of funds." The cost of funds could increase from year to year. Yet they had to cover their liability with fixed-rate mortgage assets with 30-year terms. If the cost of funds exceeded the cash they were receiving as mortgage payments, they experienced cash crunches.

Enter the adjustable-rate mortgage (ARM). Because the ARM could be indexed to the actual cost of funds experienced by the thrift, it helped to solve the mismatch of assets and liabilities.

Adjustable rate mortgages differ in the way they are indexed. Three of the most prevalent indexes are tied to the rate on Treasury securities, the London Interbank Rate (LIBOR) and the 11th District rate. The 11th District Index ties the rate on the mortgage to a formula that tries to approximate the average costs of funds to banks. The Treasury index ties the mortgage interest rate to an average of the rate on certain short-term Treasury securities. And the LIBOR index ties the mortgage rate to the rate charged by the largest European banks to each other.

It is generally agreed that, of the three most commonly used rates, the Treasury index fluctuates most rapidly, the LIBOR changes every six months or so, and the 11th District rate is the slowest. For this reason, it pays to identify the index controlling your mortgage rate.

The biggest consumer fear expressed when ARMs first were introduced concerned the potential for unlimited interest rate increases. However, ARMs usually have two types of interest rate caps. The first cap limits the amount the interest rate can increase during any one-year or six-month period. And the second cap limits the amount the interest rate can increase over the life of the mortgage. This lifetime cap typically exceeds the rate being offered for fixed-rate mortgages. One of the most common combinations of lifetime and periodic caps is the "6-2," meaning a 2 percent cap on the amount the mortgage interest rate can rise during a year and a 6 percent cap on the amount it can rise during the life of the mortgage.

Because they do not need to fear the asset/liability mismatch inherent in extending fixed-rate mortgages and because they are competitive, lenders often offer initial ARM rates substantially lower than those of fixed-rate mortgages. These "teaser" rates usually apply only to the first few years of the mortgage.

Mortgage rates also are limited by state usury laws that fix the maximum amount a lender may charge in interest. Some usury laws fix the maximum as an annual rate; others fix a maximum monthly rate or both.

Prepayment Clauses

Perhaps the most important yet overlooked provisions of a mortgage are its prepayment terms. These provisions permit you to prepay the principal of the mortgage prior to its stated term. Sometimes, the mortgage calls for you to pay a "premium" to your lender for the privilege of prepaying. Mortgages also sometimes forbid prepayment for a certain number of years, a so-called "lock-out" period.

Lenders often abhor prepayment. Prepayments deny lenders a lot of interest-laden cash flow they may have been counting on to pay liabilities.

States differ with respect to the prepayment rights lenders are required to include in mortgages. Most states view prepayment as a privilege, not a right, and your lender may not be required to give you the option to prepay. And if your mortgage is silent about prepayment, the courts will err in favor of the lender and assume you have no right to prepay. Other states have reversed the traditional view, and now, if the mortgage is silent, the presumption is that the borrower may prepay.

For example, Pennsylvania, since 1983, has taken the view that if a mortgage is silent about prepayment, the borrower is entitled to prepay. Louisiana, since 1987, and Florida, since 1988, have taken the even more liberal view that if the mortgage is silent, the borrower may prepay, without premium. Because state prepayment rules can vary so widely, if having the right to prepay is important to you, you should have your attorney review the mortgage law applicable to your mortgage as well as the particular provisions your mortgage contains.

Pros and Cons of the Fifteen-year Mortgage

Though the most prevalent mortgage has a thirty-year term, the fifteen-year mortgage is gaining in popularity. The case for the fifteen-year mortgage has strong intuitive appeal. The argument is that by paying off the mortgage in half the time, you save a whopping amount of interest. Plus, to pay the mortgage off in half the time, you do not have to make monthly payments twice as big as a comparable thirty-year mortgage. For example, paying off a 10 percent fifteen-year mortgage requires only about a 20 percent bigger monthly payment than a 10 percent thirty-year mortgage. These advantages have driven some financial advisers to sing what one writer has called a "hallelujah chorus" for the fifteen-year mortgage. As is often the case when a Great New Idea with strong intuitive appeal emerges, you now find the pendulum of popular opinion has swung almost all the way to the side of the Great New Idea, and some financial advisers have all but called those who sign on for thirty-year mortgages fools-with-pens.

But does the fifteen-year mortgage deserve such paeans? The answer, it appears, is "not always." To make a fully useful comparison of the fifteen-year and thirty-year mortgages, you must take care to identify *all* the costs involved. And when you do, you discover that the case for the fifteen-year mortgage is not so compelling as it first appears.

For example, let's assume you have a choice of taking on a 10 percent fifteen-year mortgage or a 10 percent thirty-year mortgage. Actually, since lenders usually charge a slightly higher rate for a thirty-year mortgage because their money is at risk longer, we should make the fifteen-year mortgage 9.75 percent to be more realistic. Let's further assume the mortgage is for $100,000.

The monthly payment for the fifteen-year mortgage is $1,059 for 180 payments for a grand total of $190,620. Of this amount, $90,685 represents interest.

The monthly payment for the thirty-year mortgage is $878 for 360 payments for a grand total of $316,080. Of the total, $215,925 represents interest. So, thus far, the fifteen-year mortgage would save you $125,240 in interest over the full term of the mortgage.

The difference between the monthly payment on the fifteen-year mortgage and the thirty-year mortgage is $181. If, instead of paying that extra amount to retire your fifteen-year mortgage, you invested it elsewhere, would you come out ahead? The answer depends on the profit you could earn on the alternative investment. Economists refer to the profit you can make on such alternative opportunities to use your money, aptly enough, as "opportunity costs."

Suppose you could earn 11 percent on an alternative investment during the period when you are paying off your mortgage. The extra $181, which would have been used to retire the fifteen-year mortgage, would grow to $82,298 at the end of fifteen years.

The advantages of the fifteen-year mortgage shrink even more when you consider the effects of inflation. Inflation proves the truth in the old adage that "Time is money." The effect of inflation is to erode the purchasing power of your dollars. For example, $1000 in 1990 will be worth only $995 in 1991 if inflation is 5 percent. If you look fifteen years down the line, and inflation continues to average 5 percent, the 1990 dollars will shrink in value to less than $490. Now, if you have a choice of paying off your bills with expensive 1990 dollars or relatively cheap 2015 dollars, you naturally would choose to pay off the bills with the cheaper dollars because you would save more over time. Well, the thirty-year mortgage lets you do just that by throwing cheaper dollars into the future to pay off the level monthly payment mortgage bill. By contrast, the fifteen-year mortgage throws your dollars only fifteen years into the future. You pay with the more expensive dollars and save less in real terms.

The comparison of the fifteen-year and thirty-year mortgages points out the so-called "time value of money." In effect, this concept states that the cost of using or paying money depends on the interest rate—net of inflation—that the money earns over given time periods. You should always try to bear in mind that your dollars are assets, which, like real estate, have rental value. For example, to "rent" your money, the bank pays you a rate on your savings account. Your mortgage payments are simply the rent you pay the bank for the privilege of borrowing the money used to buy the property. As long as you keep in mind that when you invest money, you deserve a certain amount of rent and when you borrow you pay a certain amount of rent, you can more easily spot circumstances in which you are being charged too much rent on the money you borrow or too little rent on the money you invest.

11. Securities

It is useful to think of securities as you do clothes. Like clothes, securities vary in complexity and function. A security can be as simple as the basic black dress or it can be as ornate and embellished as Lady Di's wedding dress. Regardless of the style or design of the security, however, to be successful it has to meet the needs of buyers. Fit enough buyers' needs, and the security becomes a classic that never goes out of style. Fit only a few buyers' needs, and the security is a one-season hit, a passing fad. In this part, we'll look at some of the classics and review a few of the fads.

But before we discuss even the merest detail about securities, before we do anything else, we must take care of what should always be the investor's most important initiation rite—loss of innocence. After your innocence is thoroughly lost, we will review some of the basic products and selection techniques all would-be buyers should understand.

Scams, Swindles, and Follies—How to Lose Your Innocence as an Investor

Loss of innocence. We have all lost innocence in one way or another. And most of us at some time have wistfully longed for the days of innocence again, be they pre-school days of playing in the sunshine, the only care in our minds what we were going to eat for lunch, or the pre-real-world innocence of living at home without paying rent, or the world before sexual liaisons. But when it comes to investing, the very last thing you should be is innocent. This chapter's goal is to help you lose your innocence voluntarily, before someone else takes it from you. For that is just what a securities fraud does—it takes your innocence; it betrays your trust and the hopes you put in a company. In the wake of fraud, you can be left bewildered and angry in addition to being poorer. Perhaps the deepest hurt is that it makes you feel just plain stupid.

Securities scams have been around for as long as securities themselves. In addition to outright fraud, there are numerous examples of investment disasters brought about by no more than innocent folly. Because ultimately your best protection against swindles is your alertness and investment memory, and because the more you know, the more alert you are apt to be, you should refer to this chapter often in your investment experience.

Before they were conquered by the Spaniards, the ancient Incas of South America had amassed unbelievable fortunes of gold and silver. One ceremony called for the planting at the feet of a chief a valley of acres of shoulder-high corn stalks. Only the corn stalks were of silver, and the thousands of corncobs, of gold. The Incas called gold "the sweat of the sun" and silver "the tears of the moon." These words seem to connect richness with the pain of acquiring it. They connect abundance with sorrow. In our society, no greater financial sorrow can befall an investor than to be had.

But you need not endure the sorrow of being tricked before you wise up enough to make smart investments. An effective shortcut is to share stories. Here are a few.

The South Sea Bubble

The South Sea Bubble scandal dates from 18th-century England, but it has lost none of its relevance over the years.

The South Sea Company was founded in 1711 to carry on a slave trade and other trade with Spanish America. At the time of the company's formation, slavery was illegal in Spain. But based on the belief that slave ownership would soon be legalized in Spain, investors flocked to South Sea Company stock. During its first six years, the company was only moderately successful.

But then fortune smiled on the company. In 1718, King George I agreed to serve as governor of the company. Investor confidence in the company soared. By 1720, investor demand for the company's stock had fanned early interest into a full-blown speculative mania.

As you know, the stories of manias about anything—teen singing idols, real estate, stock—seem to follow a kind of rhythm. The early interest is from people who genuinely are captured by the music or the cute face or the attractive neighborhood or balance sheet. These people are independently assessing the value of Donny Osmond or a house or a share of IBM in their lives and making fairly clear-eyed assessments. Then, as interest grows, the momentum draws in more of a different sort of crowd. These are the people who, on their own, would not have thought Donny Osmond was cute or that that house was perfect or that certain stock valuable, but who, seeing so many of their seemingly sane neighbors joining in the adulation, find themselves questioning their own judgment and becoming increasingly afraid of being left out of a good thing. They want to be in with the in-crowd. So they suspend their individual judgment in favor of the consensus or the collective wisdom. This I think of as the middle stage. Then comes the final stage. The final stage draws in the most desperate fringe, the true speculators. They don't care about living in the house. They know a sure thing when they see one, they assert, and they know someone else will pay twice what they are paying for it. They may even buy the house, sight unseen, at a price unthinkably high just a short time ago. They jump pell mell into the mania even at the outrageous end because they have surrendered their judgment to the belief that This Thing Will Never End.

Back to the story. After the king got involved, the mania entered the never-never land of This Thing Will Never End. The company's officers got caught up also. So confident was the company of its golden future that it proposed (and Parliament accepted) to assume a large part of England's national debt. The price of a share soared from 128 1/2 pounds in January of 1720 to over 1,000 pounds by August, just eight months later.

Everybody was in. From noblemen in fine purple silks to footmen in coarse wool, everyone had a piece of the action. People borrowed to get in. People swindled to get in. But then, our old friend reality intervened again. It became known that the laws in Spain prohibiting slavery were not going to be repealed. There would be no place to sell the slaves brought over from new conquered lands. No market, no profit. The bubble burst.

In September, a stupefied nation began to awake from a two-year binge. How horrible the atmosphere must have been, as morning's reality burned away the mist of optimism surrounding the sure thing, revealing nothing there. That fall the price of the shares continued to plummet, and by December they were trading at around 124.

The ZZZZ Best Story

If idle hands do the devil's work, then Barry Minkow, even as a boy, was an angel. His hands were always busy. In 1981 while still a teenager, Minkow started ZZZZ Best, a carpet cleaning service, in his parents' garage. His was an enchanting American success story. The company was an immediate success and, just four years after start-up, had done so well that Minkow could afford to buy a $698,000 home in California, a red Ferrari, and even a miniature poolside home with vaulted ceiling for his dog.

But Minkow wanted more. He wanted to expand. He wanted to reach the money in wallets and purses across America. And like many entrepreneurs before him, Minkow enlisted Wall Street's help to reach those national wallets and purses. In Wall Street's lingo, "he went public." Fueled by the expectation of profits from lucrative carpet-cleaning contracts, the company's stock quadrupled from $4 a share to $18 a share, creating enormous paper wealth for Minkow.

There was only one catch to the story. The lucrative carpet-cleaning contracts were more illusion than reality. In fact, Minkow later admitted that around 90 percent of the $43 million in contracts reported to investors was non-existent.

How did he get away with it? He faked documents and staged phone calls, creating a world based on lies. To explain why he defrauded so many investors, Minkow maintains he was forced to swindle by organized crime figures who supposedly beat him into cooperating.

Those who invested in Minkow's company were left wondering where the money went. Certainly some of it went to maintain Minkow's lavish lifestyle. Minkow is now in prison serving time for securities fraud. Though this undoubtedly is some salve to wounded investors, it still does not replace the money—and trust—lost.

It pays to bear in mind that not all investors in ZZZZ Best were lay people. Wall Street also was fooled. The ZZZZ Best story is a reminder that even some of the most sophisticated investment bankers on Wall Street can be defrauded by smoke and mirrors.

But even Minkow's scam is dwarfed by the schemes of Thomas Quinn.

Thomas Quinn

What's in a name? Thomas Quinn knew the importance of a name. He started his biggest swindle in the '80s by forming corporations with few or no assets, so-called "shell" companies. He then registered the shells in Liechtenstein or Switzerland. Next, Quinn hired high-pressure sales people to work the phones out of boiler rooms set up in the United States. Quinn's style was to give these boiler room operations the fanciest, most impressive-sounding names he could think of, names such as Falcon Trust, Prudentrust, and Gibraltar Financial Consultants. From these boiler rooms, Quinn's sales people made call after call to investors all over the world, hawking the stocks of the shell companies. Their particular prey were investors from the Middle East, Hong Kong, and Australia. Many of the victims were reported to have been retirees living on fixed incomes and having little experience in the stock market.

Before it was over, the final count showed that Quinn and his associates had defrauded investors of more than $500 million. Quinn used part of his take to set himself up in a lavish $6 million pink-colored villa overlooking Cannes in the south of France. As a matter of fact, Quinn was in this idyllic pink hideaway when the authorities closed in on him to arrest him in 1988.

Like many securities criminals, Quinn practiced a lot. The boiler room swindle was not his first. The Securities and Exchange Commission (SEC) had in fact barred Quinn for life from doing business with any broker or dealer as a result of other, earlier frauds. In one of these earlier scams, for example, Quinn had promoted investment in a company called Kent Industries by convincing people the company had vast real estate holdings in Florida, when in truth the company had almost no assets. Well, practice makes perfect, and if Quinn had not been caught, undoubtedly he would have added many others to his list of victims. To paraphrase an SEC commissioner, perpetrators of securities frauds are notorious recidivists.

The Sweet Little Old Lady Down the Street

Elaine Stouber of Brooklyn, New York, has the kind of warm, generous personality that draws people to her like children to a grandmother's bosom. Elaine, in the words of reporter William Glaberson, "always seemed to be there when people needed help." For years she ran a neighborhood charity. She was an aide to the man who became city council president and Brooklyn borough president. She went out of her way to worry over neighbors when they hit hard times. She won awards for outstanding community service. She was a woman you believed you could trust.

So when Elaine and her husband, Frank Aprigliano, began to solicit money for what she called a "no risk" investment plan, her neighbors naturally opened their purses to this woman who had opened her heart to them so many times before. Miriam Torren, a schoolteacher, invested her life savings of $76,000. Miriam's relatives put in another $70,000. Eileen Prucker, a housewife, and nine of her friends invested $250,000. Naomi Slomowitz and her husband had not saved a fortune during their twenty-eight-year marriage, but what they had—$28,000—they handed over to Elaine. Some of them were, of course, a little worried about investing all they had, but these fears could not stand up to their trust in Elaine. And besides, nobody wanted to miss out. As Naomi said, "Maybe this is the opportunity of my life."

Because of Elaine's apparent political connections—in addition to her borough connections, she had a big picture of herself with the governor, and she told everyone that Frank had worked for thirty-four years in a high level United Nations post—Elaine's plan seemed plausible to those who knew her. Their money, which totalled $3.9 million, would be invested in a high-yielding project to rebuild Brussels, Belgium.

For a while, Elaine's investment plan delivered. Everyone got fat interest checks. Little did they know that the fat checks were being paid not by earnings from the Brussels project but from other investors' money. When things started to unravel, Elaine's neighbors discovered to their horror that there was no Brussels project. There were no political connections with the governor. There was not even a United Nations job for Frank: he had only been a clerical worker in the United Nations' publications office. And what of their $3.9 million? Gone, all of it.

Though in 1990 they pleaded guilty in federal court to defrauding their friends and neighbors of their life savings, Elaine and Frank, to this day, maintain that they, too, were victims. Though few believe their story, they maintain they were victimized by mysterious loan sharks. Perhaps more tellingly, Elaine explained her actions to a neighbor she had swindled by confiding, "I was more desperate than you."

Investor Protection

No one can devise an investor protection system invincible to swindlers. However, there are practices that, if followed diligently, can help to lower your chances of getting taken.

The key to the success of most swindles is the simple fact that the schemers have all the information about the enterprise while the investors have comparatively little. Many investors are geographically remote from the production facilities of the company in which they are investing. As a result, there is no opportunity to verify firsthand the quality—

or even the existence—of the product or service. There is no opportunity to kick the tires.

But how do you kick the tires? How do you go about checking out a company before you put your money on the line? The best protection you have is your big, beautiful brain. Use it to understand as much as you can about the products being sold.

Just What Is a Security?

The basic idea of the security is an interest in an enterprise for profit. Then what makes a security any different from an interest in a lemonade stand? Very little, in some respects.

If three neighborhood kids decide to run a lemonade stand, they, like any other enterprise, will need two things: someone to run the stand and money to buy the initial lemons and sugar. That is, they'll need management talent and capital. At the end of a profitable day, the three kids normally will split the profits three ways, after putting aside enough money to buy additional supplies for the next day's sales. The money set aside for the next day's sales is working capital.

If, after a few weeks, the stand becomes phenomenally successful, the kids may expand their working hours or even hire other kids to run additional stands. They may even dream, if they are especially ambitious kids, of expanding citywide or into other states. But, as you can see, the growth of the stand will be limited by their ability to keep their operations under control while at the same time funding the expansion from working capital produced by daily sales. If the kids could sell interests in the stand not just to relatives and neighbors but also to interested investors states away, they could grow much faster. This is the basic bright idea behind securities. By enabling enterprises to sell interests in themselves or borrow based on their financial strength, and to do this by drawing from a geography and pool of financial resources broader than their immediate circle, securities ease operations and expansion, producing greater profits.

The development of the idea of a security changed the notion of who runs an enterprise and for whose benefit it is run. When there are only three kids and a neighborhood stand, the concept of ownership is straightforward. The kids own the stand. But as they expand, they may sell off parts of the company to investors, leaving the kids with a smaller fraction of a much bigger enterprise. And if in expanding to become the national conglomerate, Lemonade, Inc. (Lemons R' Us?), they have diluted their ownership to only 2 percent, with the remaining thousands of shareholders owning 98 percent, who now should run the company and for whose benefit?

True ownership now has shifted to a pool of largely anonymous investors who do not actually run the lemonade stands, who in fact may know nothing about running a stand, and who have little day-to-day control over the enterprise. So, though the running of the company for practical reasons remains in the hands of a few, those few now have acquired duties of loyalty and care to the anonymous thousands. They owe it to the anonymous thousands to run the enterprise as honestly and as well as they can. In legal terms, the three kids have become "fiduciaries" with "fiduciary duties."

As the number of investors grows, as the enterprise expands geographically, as the control of the enterprise separates more and more from the true owners, the more likely a court will find that the interest is a security.

Securities represent your interest in the issuing company. Your interest can be as an owner or as a creditor. If your interest is an ownership interest, the security is an equity security such as stock. If your interest is as a creditor, your security is a debt obligation such as a bond.

Basic Kinds of Securities

Securities can be divided into numerous categories. Each category should be thought of as a separate question you should pose in your analysis of a security prior to making an investment.

Among other ways, securities may be grouped according to whether they are:

1. public or private

2. debt or equity

3. government or corporate

4. rated or unrated

5. single-class or multiple class

Securities also may be categorized by whether they:

6. entitle you to special rights against the issuing company

7. have credit enhancements

Public\Private

Securities differ according to whether they are traded publicly or privately. Public securities are those issued by companies or entities that have registered the securities with the Securities Exchange Commission (SEC). Investors in public securities are entitled to the benefits of registration of the securities—mainly the right to receive certain disclosures required by the federal securities laws. The typical disclosure document for public securities is a prospectus. Through numerous regulations and court cases, the SEC has established standards of completeness and accuracy for the kind of information an issuer must include in a prospectus. All securities listed on national exchanges, such as the New York Stock Exchange, the American Stock Exchange, or over-the-counter securities, are public securities. In addition to exchange-listed securities, all United States government securities (and munis) are public securities.

Private securities are any securities that are not registered with the Securities Exchange Commission. The disclosure document accompanying private securities often is the "private placement memorandum" or PPM. The difference between the kind of information you are likely to receive in a PPM versus the information you are entitled to receive in a prospectus, as well as the advantages and disadvantages to a company of issuing public rather than private securities, are discussed later in the context of a broader discussion of the policies motivating the enforcement of the federal securities laws.

Some investors mistakenly believe that public companies issue only public securities. In fact, public companies, meaning companies that have been registered with the SEC, may issue private securities. The mere fact that a public company issues a security does not magically transform that security into a public security. The important point to remember is that it is the registration of the security, not the company, that determines whether the security is public or private. And to become public, the security itself must be registered.

For example, Donald Trump's company is a private company. But it bought the Taj Mahal Casino through the issuance of public bonds. And though the technical issuing entity may have been registered with the SEC, the creditworthiness of the private company, the Trump Organization, held the deal together.

Debt\Equity

A *debt security* represents a loan from the investor to the issuing company. In effect, you, the investor, are the lender and the company is your borrower. Common debt securities include debentures, bonds and Treasury securities.

Most of the factors you would consider important in deciding whether to lend money to anyone apply equally to your decision to invest in debt securities. Debt securities have many of the features you would expect in any loan. For example, the payoff to the investor comes in the form of interest, the security has a maturity date, the issuer typically must pay a late penalty if it fails to make timely payment of principal or interest, and the investor under some circumstances can declare the security in default.

An *equity security* represents ownership. Equity securities include common stock as well as many forms of pass-through securities. Equity securities may be further categorized according to whether they represent ownership in the company or in specific assets of the company. Because as an equity securityholder you own part of the company, you are not guaranteed success or failure, and your investment may soar to many multiples of its initial value or drop to nothing. All of us have heard of the spectacular growth of companies such as Xerox, Apple Computer, and IBM. Early investors in these companies have reaped fortunes.

Government or Conventional

Government securities carry the promise of the United States to pay them according to their terms. These securities are said to be backed by the "full faith and credit of the United States," and thus are considered the safest of all securities. The capital markets view the failure of the federal government to pay off on a promise as an unthinkable possibility. Though this prospect may have become more thinkable in these days of defaults of the massive scale involved in the savings and loan crisis, the federal government still has never defaulted in the payment of principal and interest due on any of its securities. If the Treasury runs out of cash, the thinking is that the government would print more dollars, and risk increasing inflation, or increase taxes, and therefore risk political damage, before it would allow the unprecedented market chaos that would result from such a default.

Other government securities are issued by states or local governmental entities. These are backed by the promises of the governmental authority issuing them. From time to time, fears abound that a state or city will not be able to make good on its securities. Because states and cities, unlike the federal government, do not have the option of printing money, the possibility of default is more real than is the case with federal government securities. Still, the performance of these securities has been excellent, and they are viewed, on the whole, as very safe. Since they carry the added benefit in most cases of an exemption from local taxation, the yield also can be especially attractive when compared with other near-cash alternatives.

Non-government securities are called conventional. The major category of conventional securities is corporate securities. As the name denotes, these are issued by corporations. Their safety is as good as the promise of the corporation backing them. Because they are viewed as a group as less safe than government securities, corporate securities usually offer higher yields than government securities.

Rated or Unrated

To say a security is "rated" means it has been assigned a rating by one of the companies in the business of judging the credit quality of securities. Standard and Poors (S&P), Moody's Investors Services, Inc. (Moody's), Duff & Phelphs, and Fitch Investors Services, all are major agencies, with S&P and Moody's being viewed as the leaders. Ratings agencies rank securities according to many criteria, and the criteria vary depending on the type of security involved. There is also a noticeable difference between the ratings philosophies of the various agencies. Some are more conservative in their ratings approaches for certain kinds of securities. You should become familiar with the basic mechanics the agencies use to arrive at their ratings.

Special Rights

Certain securities carry special rights against the issuing company. These rights can greatly enhance the value of the security by reducing its riskiness or increasing its profitability. For example, some securities carry the right to sell or "put" the security back to the company under certain circumstances. Another special right the security may carry is the right to exchange the security for a different security of the company. These so-called "conversion rights" may, for example, allow an investor to exchange debt securities for an equivalent value of equity securities at a certain time in the future.

Credit Enhancements

Securities may also differ according to whether the transaction that created the security gives the investor special buffers against financial reverses. One type of credit enhancement is a letter-of-credit. In certain bond deals, for example, the bond is enhanced by the presence of a letter-of-credit issued by a bank in favor of the investors. In some deals, the investors draw on the letter-of-credit from the bank if the issuing company does not pay the principal and interest when due. In other deals, the investors need not wait until the company fails to pay and can simply draw directly on the letter-of-credit. Another type of credit enhancement is the reserve fund. Some types of transactions have more than one credit enhancement, with the various buffers acting as first, second, third, and so on in lines of defense against disaster.

Common Stock—The Basic Black Dress

Z Corporation needs money. You are the vice president put in charge of the project to raise the money. The money is needed for a project crucial to Z's future—building a new state-of-the-art mainstream computer plant. You and twelve other vice presidents caucus around a mahogany table to brainstorm. You first decide:

- how much money the project requires

- how much the money will be needed

- whether the money will be needed all at once or whether staggered amounts will do

- how much the company can afford to pay to get the money

Someone suggests drawing down on one of Z's existing credit lines it maintains with its bank. But this idea is nixed because the interest on the line of credit is currently too high. Someone else suggests going to the existing bank or a new bank and getting a loan at the somewhat lower current market interest rate. But this idea also is nixed because the market rate is still higher than Z can afford to pay right now. Besides, banks ordinarily require collateral, and Z does not want to tie up its collateral for the length of time the banks would require.

You suggest that Z might raise the money from the public. Now there's an idea. It occurs to you that there are only two ways to raise money from the public. You can either borrow against Z's assets or general credit standing by issuing a debt security, or you can sell a part of Z to the public, in effect making the public a part owner, by issuing an equity security. All means of using securities to raise money from the public involve issuing some version of debt security or equity security or some combination of both.

The consensus around the table is to sell a part of the ownership. The vehicle for consummating that transaction is the basic equity security, common stock.

Selling a part of the ownership of the business has its advantages. Unlike with a borrowing, there are no creditors, no due dates, no late penalties if Z misses a payment date. Issuing common stock in the entire corporation also has its advantages over selling off specific assets of the company. After issuing common stock, Z still retains the full use of its assets. It is not required to transfer any of its hard assets to a new owner. For example, if you buy 20 percent of Z's stock, the stock does not entitle you to certain computers Z may use in its operations or certain real estate or certain desks. Instead, you would be deemed to own an undivided share of the value of the business; if all Z's assets, both tangible and intangible, are added together and expenses and liabilities subtracted, a 20 percent stockholder would own 20 percent of the total bottom line value. You would receive your profit on a yearly (or other) basis from the corporation when it declares dividends.

But being an owner in a corporation is different from being an owner of other business forms. Unlike general partners in a partnership or an owner of a sole proprietorship, owners of stock have little or no control over the management of the company. The decision making in the company is the domain of its executive officers, subject to the control of the trustees with respect to the broad direction of the company. Stockholders exercise control through their representatives on the board. If they are displeased with a certain decision of the company, they typically are not in a position to do anything to prevent the action from taking place, though they may be able to prevent such actions from taking place in the future if they act loudly and decisively to make their views known, and vote in sufficient numbers to enforce their views.

Stockholders also have little or no control over whether and when they will be paid their dividends. The decision whether and when dividends will be paid—like most other management decisions affecting the corporation—is considered the domain of the corporation's officers and directors, not its stockholders. Therefore, in the case of common stock, the purchase should be viewed as a vote of confidence in a company's management and financial policies. Moreover, if you care more about the regular income stream from dividends than about capital appreciation, you should check on the company's past performance in paying dividends before investing.

The advantages to the purchaser of stock ownership are numerous, and some of these reasons have been detailed above. A final big advantage is that a stockholder reaps all the financial benefits of ownership but escapes the unlimited liability. The stockholder thus has a chance to have her cake and eat it too. She can share in the sometimes spectacular wealth created when a company like Z grows profitable. But if Z gets hit by misfortune, such as a billion dollar lawsuit judgment, the stockholder's losses are limited to the value of her shares. Her other assets—home, bank accounts, stock in other companies—are not vulnerable to Z's bad luck.

Debt Securities: An Overview

Debt securities represent the issuing company's promise to repay. They are IOUs. The IOU can be unsecured—meaning it is backed only by the company's willingness and ability to repay. Or, the IOU can be secured in some way by the assets of the company, such as real estate or cashflow from a certain project. For secured IOUs, in effect, the company is saying, "If I don't repay, you can have my pledged asset."

A *debenture* is an issuer's unsecured IOU. A bond is an example of a secured IOU.

The distinction between unsecured and secured debt is especially critical in the event the issuer goes bankrupt. In bankruptcy, creditors are ranked according to a certain priority. Those high in priority are paid first. Secured creditors, such as certain bondholders, have claims against specific pledged assets, while unsecured creditors are paid only from the issuer's general assets remaining after the secured claims have been satisfied. As a result, unsecured creditors may ultimately receive only a small fraction of their claims, perhaps a few cents for each dollar they have invested.

As with any loan, the debenture's terms reflect the expectations of both parties. The principal amount of the loan, the interest, the deadline for repaying the loan, and late-payment penalties all are typical debenture terms.

In deciding whether to purchase a debenture, you should conduct an analysis almost identical to that made by a bank loan officer. Your goal should be to evaluate the likelihood that the issuing company will repay its IOU.

The factors you should consider include:

1. Whether the company has a good and preferably long history of repaying its debts in full and on time

2. Notwithstanding the past history of the company, whether the company is presently healthy enough financially to warrant taking on the debt in question

3. Any other indications, intangible or tangible, of the will-ingness and ability of the company to repay its debts. For instance, is the company when pressed likely to sue its creditors rather than cooperate to work out a payment plan?

You also have to consider the amount of interest being paid. Is it high enough when compared with other invest-ments competing for your dollar?

There is one important way in which you as an investor in debentures are unlike a bank making a loan. While a bank is free to negotiate the terms of its loans, typically debentures brought to the retail market have already been fully negotiated. At the point when you would be able to buy, they are take-it-or-leave-it propositions.

From the issuer's point of view, the decision to issue debentures will have been made after reviewing the alter-native costs of borrowing in the marketplace, such as the costs of taking out a bank loan. Another factor that may heavily influence the issuer's decision to issue debt securities to the public, rather than obtaining a loan from its bank, is personal liability. That is, for some multi-million-dollar loans, such as those to a private corporation domi-nated by one person, many bankers would require the head to guarantee all or part of the loan personally. This is especially true where the corporation is really the alter-ego of the man or woman who is the controlling shareholder, and the corporation's fortune is tantamount to the individual's fortune.

By contrast, an issuance of securities to the public typical-ly does not involve such a guarantee. And, because heads of corporations are human beings, given the choice between putting themselves personally on the line for mil-lions of dollars in debt or issuing debt to the public, many executives opt to go the public route.

The downside of issuing debt to the public, again from the issuer's point of view, is that such an issuance is subject to SEC scrutiny. Most private and all public debt securities are issued pursuant to a document describing the terms of the debt, called an indenture. Typical indenture terms include the promise to repay, the existence of late penalties, the circumstances constituting default, and so on. However, for public securities, the form of indenture is controlled by a federal statute, The Trust Indenture Act of 1939. This act requires the indenture to conform to guidelines of accuracy, mandates the inclusion of certain protective covenants, and requires that the indenture appoint an impartial trustee to further protect investors. Though all these requirements may make the issuance bothersome to companies, they work to the investor's advantage by giving her statutory protections, which, if not met, may give her the grounds to bring a federal securities lawsuit against the issuer and also may bring the regulatory ire of the SEC down upon the issuer's head.

Basics on Bonds

Like the debenture, the bond is an issuer's IOU. But the bond IOU is collateralized by specific assets of the company. These assets may be seized by the bondholder's representatives (ordinarily a trustee) if the company fails to pay principal and interest when due.

Maturities

"Maturity" refers to the date on which the security contract calls for the issuer to repay the investment. Often the terms of a bond allow for an early retirement of the bond. Such a "call" or "redemption" feature is critical to the pricing of the bond. For example, assume you are on a fixed income and you have decided to invest $10,000 in a bond paying 10 percent per annum. Your reasoning is that even though you could make more with stocks, you need the regular quarterly stream of interest a bond will pay. But you neglected to examine the indenture, which explained that though the maturity of the bond is ten years, the bond is callable after only three years, at the option of the issuer. So, though you have invested in a ten-year bond, and you are counting on a steady stream of interest for the full ten-year period, you may be faced in three years with the prospect of reinvesting the $10,000 in an interest rate market paying only 7 percent, a substantial reduction in the interest stream you need.

The maturities of debt securities vary in length and can range anywhere from a few months to several decades. Most bonds, however, have long-term maturities.

Discount or Interest-Bearing

All debt securities are designed to pay profit in some form. How that profit is expressed, however, can vary. So-called "interest-bearing" debt securities are sold at par face value and pay interest at a coupon rate on the face value periodically. In our earlier example of a $10,000 bond paying 10 percent quarterly, $10,000 is the face value of the bond. Ten percent is the coupon rate.

Other debt securities are sold for less than par and pay full par face value at maturity. The profit you make is the difference between the amount you pay initially and the face value at maturity. These are so-called "discount" debt securities. For example, a broker may offer to sell you a bond for $9,750 paying $10,000 at the end of ten years. The hidden interest you would earn is $250.

Debt securities sold at discount often are expressed as a percentage of the full face value. For example, a discount bond trading at 99.75 percent means you would pay 99.75 percent of the full face value to buy the bond. If the discount is particularly large, say 88 percent of par, the bonds are called, aptly enough, "deep discount" bonds.

Some discount bonds pay you the amount of profit you are accruing periodically before maturity. To use the example of the ten-year discount bond purchased for $9750 yielding $10,000 at maturity, the issuer could pay your $250 profit in installments of $25 per year for the ten-year period. Other discount bonds pay no interim interest at all. You receive your profit only at maturity. These are called "zero-coupon" bonds or "zeros" for short.

Many financial planners recommend long-term zeros to save for college. A twenty-year zero purchased when your baby is still an infant would mature when the baby is in college, in time to help with tuition costs. And, because the bond is so long-term, the initial purchase price usually is affordable for most investors.

Some of you may be wondering whether the hidden interest in zeros is taxable. The answer, unfortunately, is yes. Products discounted at the time of issue (called, appropriately enough by the IRS, "original issue discount" or "OID" products) are taxed as though the interest accruing over the term of the product is paid annually, even though you may not actually receive interest until the maturity date.

Ratings

Typically, public bonds are assigned ratings by one or more of the nationally recognized ratings agencies such as Standard & Poors or Moody's. These ratings are arrived at by analysts at the ratings agencies who test the hypothesis that the bond's principal and interest will be timely paid. They test the issuer's ability to stay current on the bond's payments by looking at various likely and worst-case scenarios. They look at the issuer's historical payment record and the health of the issuer's basic business as well as the structure of the transaction from which the bond is issued. But before you buy a bond or any security for that matter, do your own worst-case scenario evaluation. Kick the tires. For the mere presence of a stellar rating does not guarantee that no problems will develop. There are several famous cases of bonds (for example the aptly acronymed WHOOPS utility bonds) that had the highest ratings only a year before they tanked. As much as practically possible, *do not use ratings as substitutes for your own homework.* Use them only to confirm what your brain discerns.

Junk Bonds

As we noted earlier, the lowest categories of speculative products include investments with significant risk that the debtor will default on its IOU. Junk bonds, you may think, all fall into this category. Actually, the pendulum of conventional wisdom has now swung all the way to the negative side on junk bonds. But what is or is not junk depends a lot on how closely you look at the products. In today's atmosphere, any bond that is not investment grade is labeled, sometimes too hastily, as junk. It turns out that not all junk is junk. Some bonds that newspapers may brand as junk actually are just below investment grade and present no significant risk of going into default. These bonds pay significantly higher interest rates than investment grade bonds, and, in some cases, the higher interest rates more than justify the increased risk of default. And on closer inspection, what you find is that the monolithic term "junk bond" actually covers a broad range of products displaying a range of riskiness. Wait a minute, you may ask—should I run out and invest in junk bonds? No. All we're doing is pointing out that if your portfolio is suitable for a managed degree of speculative risk, certain bonds labeled broadly as "junk" may not in fact be so trashy. The important thing to do is to take conventional wisdom with a grain of salt and to use your own brain to identify how inherently risky a given bond truly is. Then decide what percentage of your total portfolio you should devote to speculative assets. If, for example, you will devote 2 percent of your portfolio to such speculative assets, junk bonds could fill the bill.

How to Select a Broker

Has your doctor ever gone to jail for killing a patient? Did he or she graduate from medical school? Most people, before they submit their bodies to a doctor's care or their legal fate to a lawyer's hands, want to know—or should want to know—some basic background information. Are they really licensed? Have they been sued for malpractice? Have any disciplinary proceedings been brought against them? Have they, God forbid, ever gone to jail?

These same types of questions are important when ferreting out the good broker from the bad. After all, if you use a broker, he or she is entrusted with a good deal of your financial future. If brokers are good, they can become lifelong allies against financial disaster. But if they are bad, for reasons including dishonesty or plain incompetence, they can cause the worst financial disaster ever to hit your pocketbook.

How do you check out your broker? You begin with a phone call. Most brokers are required to register with the National Association of Securities Dealers (NASD). The NASD and the North American Securities Administrators Association jointly maintain a database in Washington, D.C. (202-737-0900) containing information on brokers and financial planners supplied by each of the fifty state securities departments. The association will give you the phone numbers of state securities departments, and you may call the departments directly. Also, through its fifty-state database, called the Central Registration Depository (CRD), the association can tell you the broker's educational and employment information and whether the individual has been the subject of federal securities proceedings or whether, in connection with investments, the individual has been convicted of misdemeanors or felonies.

Unfortunately, the CRD reports only closed cases and final results. It tells you nothing about pending cases. You may be able to find out whether the broker is the subject of a pending disciplinary proceeding involving violation of state law by calling individual state regulatory agencies. You should also check with the New York Stock Exchange and other exchanges as well as dealer associations.

Though the overwhelming number of brokers never get into regulatory trouble, the NASD reports that in 1990, 464 brokers were barred or suspended. The cases ranged from the small-time—one broker stole $312—to the outrageous—some brokers stole money from clients by falsifying documents and borrowing against their client's life insurance policies. Fully 30 percent of the 464 cases involved theft of client money. Another 105 involved excessive, unsuitable, or unauthorized trades, 83 involved serious rule violations and 24 involved forgery. Clearly, you should do some serious homework before you sign up with any broker.

Part of that homework can be based on information the broker gives you. If brokers represent themselves as being affiliated with a major brokerage firm, call the firm yourself to verify this information. If they claim to be certified, call the certifying institution. Ask them for client references and follow up on the information you are given. Certainly, before you hand over your money, make sure they really are brokers.

Even those brokers selected through word-of-mouth references from family and friends should be given your standard check. For some of the most infamous swindles have been pulled by con artists whose first trusting victims spread the gospel about their homegrown financial wizard to family and friends.

Often underestimated as a factor in the selection of a financial adviser is personal chemistry. Do you sense that this person is someone you can work with closely? Do you trust him or her? Does the person put you at your ease and make you feel as though your questions are worthwhile? Or do you feel, even slightly, as though the broker regards your questions as stupid? Do you detect arrogance?

My first experience in selecting a broker was memorable. I walked into the offices of a branch of a well-known brokerage house. The receptionist, who wore her hair bobbed and pinned behind her ears in one of those underjoyed constructions designed to make her look ten years older than her age, was the first barrier. She looked me over, then ushered me to a spot and told me to wait while she found a broker. Most brokerage houses have a broker-of-the-day assigned to handle walk-ins and people like me who do not have the name of a specific broker to see. We walk-in traffic types clearly were not held in great esteem because I stood there for half an hour, unnoticed amid a blur of phone conversations and people bumping me as they rushed papers from one cubicle or office to another. The room seemed to have a pulsing rhythm, and I was clearly off the beat. Like a palm tree planted in the middle of traffic, I was an object moving cars swerved around, not because they feared cutting my bark but because they did not want to bend a fender. Finally, one of the cars noticed me, slowing down as he approached.

He was a sleek, new, neon-red, sporty two-seater with Brooks Brothers safety belts holding up his trousers and fashionably-hidden headlights. The horned-rimmed lids uncovered his headlights, revealing two bright, just-graduated eyes. His V-8 engine purred in a profession-al, low growl. "Hi, my name is Mark So-and-So. May I help you?" Mark was the broker-of-the-day, assigned to handle walk-ins. I told Mark I wanted to talk about a com-pany I had heard about that made software used to forecast sales. He was immediately enthusiastic and wanted to put me "in" for 100 shares at $15 a share. Then I asked about the company's earnings history. Uh, yes, he did have the earnings history of course and could send it to me in about a week, but first I should really buy now before the price went any higher. Since I dearly loved my meager savings, I decided to wait the week until I got the earnings report in hand. Somewhere, a button on a dashboard was pushed, and the lids came down again over Mark's headlights. "Well, call me when you are serious about buying, and I will be happy to help."

There is a fundamental truth about brokers, which, if faced early, will save you a lot of misery and help you select one best for you. Unless they are on high salaries—few are—brokers make their money from commissions earned when they buy or sell. They only make money when shares change hands. If you are not planning to be active in the market and have a sufficiently large portfolio to warrant trading, you are not really a profitable prospect for them. You are a tree.

If you are a tree who perhaps wants to buy and hold shares, nothing fancy, then make sure you land in a forest and not a traffic jam. Your search should be for a broker who is willing to go slow enough to guide your selections objectively and patiently. Make sure you have found one who cares about trees.

Brokers are either full-service or discount. Full-service firms charge more money and justify the higher charges by pointing out their extensive research capabilities. They are selling you access to information and guidance. If, on the other hand, you want to go it alone and rely on your own ability to select securities for your portfolio, you may choose among the hundreds of discount brokers. Discount brokers just do what you tell them. You make the selections.

Bear in mind that not all brokers—full–service or discount—charge the same. Most compete ferociously to distinguish themselves from the others, and there can be considerable variation in commissions charged. But whether you use a full-service firm or a discount broker, you have to know which selection techniques to follow. For even if you are using a full-service broker, you want his or her philosophy of securities selection to match yours.

Life with Stocks—Selection Techniques

Sometimes, reading financial literature about stock selection leaves you with a feeling they are talking to aliens. The clinical, seemingly rational advice they give just does not seem to matter. You remember your own harrowing, fingernail-biting rollercoaster ride with stocks. Real life is rarely a rational experience.

When you are sitting on top of a shrinking portfolio that has got to fund your retirement plans and tuition for the kids, the last thing you need is cold, clinical, you're-stupid-for-being-scared advice. What you need is a fellow nail-biter to assure you that if you'll stick to your plan and resist bad habits, resist panicking at any rate, there really is a good ending to the story.

Before we get to the good ending, however, let me offer my nail-biting credentials. Today, as I write this chapter, an article appeared in *The New York Times* announcing that, yes, folks, the long bull run of the 1980s is over and it is time to let the crying commence. We are officially in a bear market.

How does an official bear market feel? If you are over 18, you have already encountered one or more bears. One of the mutual funds I have invested in has lost 10 percent of its value since the start of the year. The fund has an 800-number. One night in October, I called the number (I have resisted calling during the first nine months of the year because I knew the news would not be good) and spoke with an account representative.

"Hello, my account number is so-and-so and I'd like to know the current market value of the so-and-so fund."

"Just one minute, mam. . . . O.K. . . . you currently have so-and-so number of shares."

"Excuse me, I didn't want the number of shares (I never keep up with the number of shares until I compare statements every three months or so). Just give me the current dollar value of my holdings."

He tells me the figure. My stomach feels tight, and I am getting angry. The anger is not rational. After all, none of these fund managers *wants* to lose money. Besides, this rep is not responsible. But they are trained to hold the hands of nervous customers to keep us from doing something rash, like cashing out. I am badly in need of some hand-holding. I try another tack.

"Uh, what happened? I know the market's down. The economy's slowing. Iraq invaded Kuwait and so on. But what is Mr. So-and-So (naming the fund manager) doing about positioning the portfolio to improve performance?"

"What do you mean by that?" says the account representative.

My stomach tightens a bit more. My reaction has nothing to do with what he is saying. It is his tone of voice. That damned practiced cheerfulness. I am feeling it, the pain of lost money, and this guy is cheerful. I shift into a lawyer's tone.

"What I mean is that the market's going down. Everybody knows that. But my fund pays Mr. So-and-So a fee on the belief that his presence matters. If the effect of his management is that our fund is going down as much or more than the market, there is not a whole lot of sense in paying him—or you for that matter."

There is silence on the other end of the phone for a moment. I realize I have crossed the line of civility with this guy. His retaliation. Even more cheerful-speak. He thanks me for my comments and we hang up.

What is the soundest strategy to follow? Hold on to the fund shares? Cash out? Switch to another fund? The strategy I followed was to hold on to my shares. Why? Because the reason I bought the shares was for a long-term investment in the market. This money would be needed in about fifteen years. The stocks underlying the mutual fund shares would not come into their own even in the best of economic times for another five years or so. I opted for patience and long-term strategy. I swallowed some pretty bad-tasting nervousness in doing so. But the strategy has worked for me and millions of others in the past and there is no reason to believe that it will not work now, given that the key management and financial strength of the market sectors in which the fund has invested have not changed.

In fact, the overall move I make is to invest a fixed amount in each of the common stock funds I have selected each month. I did this even as Iraq invaded Kuwait sending the world's oil markets into chaos, even as the recession appeared to deepen, and even as the consensus in the newspapers emerged that indeed we were in for a prolonged bear market. I do this simply because it is the smartest move for the long term.

The rationale of this strategy is the concept of *dollar cost averaging*. Some investors discovered long ago that if you invest a fixed amount in stocks on a periodic basis, in my case monthly, you come as close as you can to a "no-lose" strategy. Say you invest $100 a month in the shares of Z corporation. In January Z shares are trading at $20 per share, so your monthly investment buys you five shares of Z for January. In February, Z's share price rises to $25 per share, so your investment buys you four shares. And in May the share price falls precipitously to $10, so your investment buys you ten shares. As you can see, as Z's share price increased, you ended up buying fewer shares. The effect is that you are always positioned to make the smartest move, buying more when stocks are a bargain and less when stocks are expensive. This is the beauty of dollar cost averaging.

When combined with the common sense techniques of analyzing companies according to basic fundamental attributes—is the company's product well made? Does it take on only a sensible amount of debt? Is management awake?—dollar cost averaging can position you to realize good long-term returns.

Of course, not everyone uses these selection techniques. Some of you also may not find them compelling. And while it is not necessary that you agree with me to realize good returns, it is crucial that you become clear about which strategy you are using and why. It is even more crucial to understand which strategy you favor if you are using a broker or someone else to manage your portfolio. What you may find is that you disagree with the basic theory of investing your broker follows.

According to some authorities, investing in the stock market is a simple matter: All you have to do is buy a stock when its price is too low (undervalued) and sell when the price is too high (overvalued). And at the race track all you have to do is bet on the horse that wins.

How do you know when a security is trading at a "low" or a "high"? You have seen the dollar cost averaging method I follow. Are there any other techniques for spotting highs and lows? Though the variety of methods used to value stocks seems to increase each day, it is still possible to identify four basic strategies that have dominated securities analysis for years. The strategies are fundamental analysis, technical analysis, "new investment analysis," and the random walk.

Fundamental Analysis

The best way to understand the differences between the strategies is to go back to childhood. Let's say it is Christmas Eve or the night before the first day of Hanukkah. You are awake with anticipation. You know you are getting a Western Flyer bicycle because you have spied it in its unglamorous, unassembled state in the attic. But as you lie in bed, listening to the voices in the living room, you begin to realize there is a problem. Something is going wrong with the assembly of the bike. The world is not right.

Your mother is one of those moms who believes she can figure out anything. When the TV broke, she did not shake it or smash it or wait until it came around on its own. She calmly opened the owner's manual, ignored the back panel warning "DO NOT OPEN," and proceeded to figure out what was wrong. So, it is only natural that in assembling your bicycle, she knows she can make it work. She opens the trusty owner's manual and begins to read. Hours later, she is still at work, jotting down some calculations, using a ruler to measure carefully, maybe writing on graph paper, you get the picture. This bike will work, she believes, because reason works. Reason is provable truth. And when she reaches a problem that will not yield to the laws of reason, she figures she has not reasoned enough. She is, at her core, a fundamental analyst.

The fundamental analyst reasons that every stock has a certain, discoverable, intrinsic value. If you can ascertain that value, then the decision whether to buy or sell is easy. Buy if the price is lower than that intrinsic value; sell if the stock is higher than that value. To discover that intrinsic value, the fundamental analyst assumes basically that:

$$value = (future\ earnings) \times (multiplier)$$

Why future earnings? The fundamental analyst reasons that if the stock is ever going to yield dividends or appreciate in value, the only source for the dividends or value are the company's future earnings.

The multiplier in the equation describes some of the factors that might enhance the earnings prospects of the company—management talent, consumer appetite for the company's product, and so on. Good management may mean a multiplier of 5, world class management a 10, poor management only a 1. On an industry-wide basis, analysts may speak of industry multipliers for, say, the computer industry of 15 and the steel industry of 8. Industry-wide multipliers reflect the market's assessment of the future prospects of the industry. Is the industry positioned well for the long term or is it the "hula hoop" or "pet rock" industry of the moment?

But who can predict the future? If, in estimating the present value of future income, the fundamental analyst has to embrace the inherently irrational business of forecasting the future, is then the fundamental analyst a self-delusionist? One of the most brilliant, creative thinkers Wall Street has ever known thinks so. Burton Malkiel, whose theory of random walk we discuss later, believes that fundamental analysts cannot ascertain a company's future income or stock price because they cannot possibly predict whether or how long the profits picture will be rosy. As he puts it, "God Almighty does not know the proper price-earnings multiplier for a common stock."

Buying a stock is in many ways like buying a company. The same considerations apply. After all, that is what you are doing when you buy shares, even if your purchase is relatively small. It is useful to look at how sophisticated business people buy an entire company.

Z Company is for sale. Ms. Wise and Mr. Young are considering whether to buy. They, their accountants, and lawyers review Z's balance sheets and income statements for each of the past five years and discover that in each of those years Z has produced about $1 million in after-tax earnings. How much should they pay for Z?

To determine how much to pay, they must work from the known to the unknown. They know how much Z has made. They must use this information to try to guess intelligently how much Z will make. That is, they must determine the appropriate multiplier for a company such as Z. Determining the appropriate multiple of earnings is an imprecise process, and the ultimate figure paid will be the result of a sometimes hard-fought compromise between the buyer and seller of the company, the age-old tug of supply and demand. Ms. Wise and Mr. Young, the potential buyers of Z, must consider the following questions:

1. Will Z continue to earn at least $1 million annually for the indefinite future or are there ominous clouds over the industry in general or Z in particular that should dampen these expectations?

2. What kind of multiples have been applied in the sales of other healthy businesses similar to Z?

3. What is the return on alternative uses of the money you would have to invest to buy Z? Are the alternative investments much riskier or safer than Z?

Brokers who speak of the "price-earnings multiple" or the "price-earnings ratio" are employing the same concepts as Wise and Young. The difference is that the P/E ratio is based on the price per share, not the price of the entire business.

Is the multiple Wise and Young decide on the right one? No one can predict with certainty whether Z actually will earn $1 million per year in the future. Not even the most brilliant financial guru has so clear a crystal ball.

Other commentators have offered a perhaps more damaging criticism of fundamental analysis. Because the multiple reflects the total of all information available to the public, it is not possible, they argue, to outbet the market using fundamental analysis without inside information. This criticism sometimes is referred to as the "efficient market" critique of fundamental analysis. This criticism, however, may not wholly join the argument for fundamental analysis on closer inspection. True, the multiple does reflect information some or all of which may be publicly available. However, the multiple is limited to the time horizon used in its derivation. For example, a multiple of ten may be based upon a predicted income stream of five years. If the investor believes the multiple understates the reliability and length of the income stream, it would be possible to buy at a multiple of ten, and still make a profit.

Fundamental analysis also can be used to value debt securities. Here, the basic "fundamental" is the company's ability to repay principal and interest due. The most common method used to value that ability is some form of "coverage" test. Such a test measures how many times the earnings of a company would cover the debt payments. If, for example, a company earns $1 million per year and has taken out a loan requiring a total of $100,000 in annual payments, the coverage would be ten. Expressed as a formula,

$$coverage = earnings/debt\ costs$$

Coverage tests differ with respect to what is included in the numerator and what is in the denominator. Some tests measure net income in the numerator and only the interest payments in the denominator. An even more restrictive test might put net income in the numerator and both principal and interest due in the denominator. You might select as a measure of safety the relationship the total amount of pre-tax earnings of the company over the past seven years bears to the total amount of debt incurred by the company over that same period. The resulting coverage would be a rough estimate of the company's creditworthiness.

Perhaps the best known fundamental analysts are the late Benjamin Graham and his collaborator David Dodd. In 1934, Graham and Dodd published what has now become a classic text of fundamental analysis, *Securities Analysis.* Graham has written a later book, which has become a classic in its own right, *The Intelligent Investor.* I highly recommend both. Graham and Dodd's theories have taught a generation of investors, perhaps none more successful than the legendary investor, Warren Buffet. Buffet, whose net worth is valued around $4 billion, is the quintessential fundamental analyst. He scouts for undervalued companies, follows his own good sense of whether the company is doing the basics right—like treating customers well, making a good product consistently—and invests accordingly. Buffet's company is Berkshire Hathaway, based, as is Buffet, in Omaha, Nebraska. Berkshire is diversified and many maintain that owning a single share of Berkshire is in a sense like owning a stake in a well-run mutual fund. The company often lands up on the list of best stocks to own, although recently some have suggested that at more than $8,000 per share, it is a bit overvalued.

Graham and Dodd highlighted a basic distinction between "investors" and "speculators." Investors are interested in the performance of the company over a long term. They are long-term seekers of value. They should have temperaments to weather the momentary queasiness of the market and remain patient and secure in the knowledge that a correctly analyzed stock will prove its value over time. Speculators, by contrast, are shorter term thinkers. They make their money in the quick turnover of stocks. They get impatient when results are not positive soon after they have purchased shares. We cannot moralize about whether one strategy is right and the other wrong. Some buy a house to live in forever, and others buy it to flip it in a rising market. Some buy a stock to have and hold, some to flip it quickly in a rising market. Both techniques can make money. However, flipping for a quick profit requires an exquisite sense of timing. Did you flip out too soon? What if no buyer comes around for awhile and you bought high because you were certain you could flip? Are you financially sound enough to last until a new buyer comes along? If you are one of those flippers who buys high, let's face it, your success will depend on finding the "greater fool." And, unless you have found the magical market that only goes up, you would have to possess the prodigious timing of a Flying Wallenda to flip successfully over a significant period.

Studies have shown that over any period longer than ten years, stocks have outperformed every other investment vehicle. But to take advantage of this ability of stocks to deliver good returns, you must value the stock correctly and be willing to hold it for a longer period.

Technical Analysis

Again, it is the dead of night and there is a problem getting your bicycle assembled. Only this time your mom believes not so much in reason as in the predictableness of human behavior. Very early in December, she opened the box, guessing—correctly in this case—that someone forgot to put in a part. Thus, with bicycle parts in front of her, and having failed in her first attempt to assemble it according to the owner's manual, she snaps her fingers and grimaces knowingly. "Isn't that just like human nature," she says, shaking her head, "to sell someone a bike without all the necessary parts." To decide what to do next, she searches her memory for any similar circumstances in the past. She recalls dealing with the store about a defective toaster ten years ago and getting a face full of rude remarks. The incident resulted in her having to sue the company, paying legal fees, and still not getting a new toaster. Though unbeknown to her, the management of the store has changed and all the people who dealt with her so rudely the first time around have moved on, she believes so strongly that history repeats itself that she decides not to pursue the matter with the bike. Your bike is assembled a few days later using a part bought from another store.

If the motto of the fundamental analyst is that "reason works," a fitting motto for the technical analyst is, "There's nothing new under the sun." Believing there really is nothing new, whenever the technical analyst encounters a set of events, she sets out to discover among the patterns of the past a similar set of events. Having found a matching pattern, she then extrapolates by assuming that the next future event will be just like the one that followed the events in the matching past pattern. The belief is grounded on the premise that people have always been people and since people move events, events in the past will form patterns useful in the future.

Technical analysts rely on charts of past market performance. The chart for a particularly turbulent market may, for example, look jagged, like the Manhattan skyline. A chart of a bull market may look like an ascending mountain peak and a prolonged bear market like the downside of the mountain. The search for meaning in these charts is reminiscent of the game we play as kids to identify shapes in clouds. Is that an angel's face? No, I see a German shepherd's head, and that fuzzy part sticking out is his tail.

The success of technical analysts depends greatly on understanding the market psychology, which they believe drives the lines on the charts. In effect, they try to time the market.

In the 1980s, technical analysts and their fabled charts enjoyed a nice spell of popularity, thanks to a chartist named Ralph N. Elliot, whose theories first were published in the 1930s. Studying charts of stock market movements, Elliot believed he discerned distinct patterns that repeated themselves after roughly five cycles, now called Elliot Waves. Two Elliot Wave theorists of the '80s, Robert Prechter and A.J. Frost, wrote a book predicting that the 1980s would see a rampaging bull run. Well, nothing succeeds or convinces like success, and when a bull market of gigantic dimension occurred, appearing to prove the Elliot

Wave theorists right, the theory and its gurus gained fame and followers. Some financial advisers angled to claim the glory of the success. Prechter and Frost emerged as winners of the status of modern-day parents of the rebirth of the Elliot Wave theory.

But though success has many parents, failure is an orphan. And when the Elliot Wave theorists' predictions began to falter, academics attacked the chartists ferociously, and followers abandoned the theory in droves. Today, Prechter and Frost appear to disagree on whether we are in the fourth or fifth peak of the cycle, but both seem to believe the 1990s will see a broad retrenchment. Other technical analysts believe that the '90s will see a continuation of the bull run. Investors can pay their money—services like Prechter's cost hundreds of dollars a year—and take their choice. As Major Bowes of the Original Amateur Hour said of the wheel of fortune, "Round and round and round she goes, and where she stops, nobody knows."

The Random Walk Theory

There are those who believe the nature of the market is random. Like the wheel of fortune, there is, they assert, no meaningful pattern to success in stock selection. They argue that the likelihood of future earnings cannot be predicted from the tools of the fundamental analyst or from the market psychology and charts of the technical analyst.

Random Walkers believe the tracings of ups and downs, plateaus and bell curves of the market's performance are produced by a completely random process. Were you a tiny traveler along a stock earnings curve and someone stopped you on Tuesday and asked, "Where will you be on Wednesday?" they believe the true answer you must give is, "I don't know; I haven't a clue." In fact, according to the Random Walkers, no one has a clue.

But if the walk is random, is the journey pleasureless for all but the truly aimless and the silly? The complete randomness of the market would be a hard reality to face because, if true, it would mean the market is a pure gamble. Yet such a gamble involves our retirement money, our

college endowments, indeed a large part of the capital
structure of the United States economy and the economies
of countries all over the globe. The mind rails against the
possibility that so much is left to the mathematical indifference of a dice throw.

It has been said that the human brain is incapable of
comprehending infinity. It is something like trying to think
about nothing. But to comprehend randomness we would
need to stretch our brains to the outer reaches of infinity,
for randomness predicts that certain processes carried out
an infinite number of times will produce no meaningful
pattern, even though along the way pseudopatterns appear.
For example, consider the simple game of flipping a coin.
Heads I win, tails you win. After ten tries, you may have
won seven times and I only three. After 100 times, you still
may be ahead but by a slimmer margin, say sixty-five to
thirty-five. After 1000 times, you may only be ahead 510 to
490. But the results are getting closer together because the
process of flipping a two-sided coin is random. And,
assuming the coin is not weighted in some way—it is not
heavier on one side or the hand motion of the flipper is not
biased one way or another—the odds will get closer and
closer to fifty-fifty as we get closer and closer to an infinite
number of flips.

But no one ever in practice gets to flip an infinite number
of times. Mathematically, we use statistics to approximate
the universe of infinite tries. We are able to say using statistics that such-and-such is true with a 95 percent degree of
confidence based on the size of the sample used. The larger the sample, the closer to 100 percent degree of confidence and the world of infinite tries. Random Walkers point
to studies showing that the statistical chances of beating the
market do not improve by eliminating certain kinds of risk.
They show that even diversification of your portfolio will
not reduce certain kinds of risk. The stubborn risk even
diversification will not eliminate, they say, is attributable to
random processes.

From time to time, you see stock analysts who are either
fundamental analysts or chartists trying to discredit the random walk theory by throwing darts at a board of stock

names and comparing the performance of the picks to the stocks selected by their favorite theory. The Random Walkers dismiss this kind of test, basically because it is not random (infinite, unbiased) enough.

The random walk theory comes in basically two flavors, the so-called "weak form" and the "strong form."

Weak Form of Random Walk

The weak form of the random walk theory is an attack on chartists. If you look at a significant amount of data on the market, say the Random Walkers, you will discover that plots and charts of past performance have no meaningful relationship to future performance, that a graph of performance for the last five years that looks like a sketch of the Manhattan skyline may, for the next five years, look like a sketch of the Great Plains. Lines are just lines. There is no meaning behind them. No intelligence guides them. You would do as well to produce your "chart" by dipping an ant in ink and letting it crawl across a sheet of paper.

The data amassed appears to support this criticism. The mountain of data is so high that indeed many believe technical analysis has been academically discredited.

Strong Form of the Random Walk

The strong form of the random walk theory maintains that neither technical analysis nor fundamental analysis will produce performances any better than a randomly selected portfolio. We have already dealt with the Random Walker's critique of technical analysis. The critique of fundamental analysis is based on the Random Walker's belief in the efficiency of the market. By complete efficiency what is meant is that all information both from the past and present (as well as all information knowable in the future) already has been reflected in the price of the security. Therefore, the theory goes, only the unknown and unknowable—the realm of randomness—are not reflected, putting the fundamental analysts and the Random Walker on at least an equal footing as predictors.

The Beta

Most investment strategies can be reduced to the quest for the sure thing. Scratch either a fundamental analyst or a chartist and what you will find is a human being who makes a living trying to help other human beings eliminate risk from their lives. Risk is the enemy, with its unpredictability and unmanageability.

Throughout its life, a security carries the basic risk that it will not deliver to its owner as much value as the owner expects.

What are the chances that a security will not live up to expectations? One of the ways academics answer this question is by assessing the security's "beta." The beta is a measure of the volatility of a security relative to the market. Securities with betas of 1 are considered as volatile as the market. They can be expected to go up or down more or less in tandem with the market as a whole, as measured by, say, the S&P 500 market index. Securities with betas less than 1 are considered less volatile than the market, and securities with betas greater than 1 are more volatile than the market.

Analysts expect securities with high betas to be jittery. High betas are expected to overreact. If the market gets a cold, high betas get the flu. If the market is happy, high betas are ecstatic. You would also expect that since more risk should bring a chance of greater return, if you invest in a jumpy stock, you should get higher returns than investors in a relatively predictable stock. However, reality again thumbs its nose at theory's perfect world: the studies just do not bear out this relationship between jitteriness and return. The data does not show that stocks with high betas outperform calmer stocks over a significant period.

Mechanics of Buying and Selling

There are four basic ways to transfer a security through an exchange:

1. buy

2. sell

3. sell "short"

4. sell "short against-the-box"

To effect these transfers, you can use one of four kinds of orders:

1. market orders

2. limit orders

3. buy-stop orders

4. sell-stop orders

There are two ways to pay for the transaction:

1. cash

2. credit using a margin account

Buying and Selling

Say Barbara buys 10,000 shares of Z at $5 per share, paying $50,000 cash. Then she sells the stock, realizing a profit or a loss. Barbara has engaged in an ordinary buy and sell transaction.

Selling Short

Selling short means Barbara is selling stock she does not own. Here is how it works. Barbara believes Z stock is going to fall in price. She instructs her broker to borrow 10,000 shares of Z. She then contracts to sell the 10,000 borrowed shares at today's price of $50,000. So far, so good. She's got $50,000. But now she has to return the shares she borrowed. She waits until the price of Z falls to, say $4 per share. Then she fulfills her obligation to return the 10,000 borrowed shares by buying the shares in the market, using $40,000 of the $50,000 she made when she initially sold Z. She nets a nice profit of $10,000 before broker's commissions.

Nice work, if you can time it. Now let's suppose things do not go quite as well as expected. This time, Barbara again bets that Z's shares are going to fall. She borrows 10,000 shares and sells them at $5 a share for a total of $50,000. Then she has to return the borrowed shares. So she instructs her broker to buy 10,000 shares of Z at market price. Only, this time, she guessed wrong. Instead of falling, Z's share price has risen by a dollar to $6 per share. Since Barbara must return the borrowed shares, she must cover the short by spending $60,000 to buy the 10,000 shares. Now, $50,000 of the $60,000 comes from the money she got when she sold the borrowed shares. She was in effect playing with someone else's money. The other $10,000 comes out of Barbara's pockets.

As you can see, the danger in selling short is that the market will move away from you too fast for you to cover your position. How much time do you have to cover? When do you have to return the borrowed shares?

Most brokerage houses have the same procedures for opening accounts to trade shorts and for covering shorts. The uniformity is explained in large part because the rules governing margin accounts are set by the SEC. Brokerage houses have certain maintenance requirements applicable to short accounts. These rules require you to maintain a certain amount of equity in the account and to make up the deficit in the account as the market moves away from you. Since you make money in a short account if the stock price falls, the house will let you keep your short position open as long as you are making a profit. You can, of course, close the position and take the profit at any time. But as the share price climbs, you start losing money. The brokerage house then requires you to deposit cash to stabilize your position.

Short sales rely on timing and credit to make you a profit. And though just the thought of making money when the stock is falling may seem irresistible, the chance you take that the market will move against you can be ruinous. Remember that one of the things you could count on in investing in stocks is that you can only lose what you put in. Not so, with a short sale. Because you are gambling with what you do not own, you may have to pay what you do not have.

Rather than getting her relatively cheap inventory of stock from the markets, Barbara, if she already owned Z stock cheaper than the market, could effect a special kind of short sale, called a short "against-the-box." Basically, Barbara could sell Z short, then replace the borrowed shares with shares she already owns. The practice of selling short against-the-box is not new. It has been around for at least fifty years. In fact, during the Congressional debates surrounding the passage of the major federal securities laws in the 1930s, congressmen railed against the practice, calling it a means for corporate insiders to conceal dealings in the stock of their corporations. One congressman was so vehement against short-selling in general and against-the-box practices in particular that he vowed he would "not desist until these invidious and thoroughly reprehensible practices" were abolished.

Undoubtedly, part of the anger against short selling grew out of the knowledge that short sellers profited while those investing in the company's growth—and indeed the entire post-Crash nation—suffered. It probably is the same sort of barely disguised anger we have towards funeral directors and vultures.

Orders

As noted above, there are four kinds of orders that you may have executed through an exchange:

1. market orders

2. limit orders

3. buy-stop orders

4. sell-stop orders.

A market order from Barbara instructs her broker to buy or sell the security at the best price available in the market. The market order "buy Z" means to buy Z at the lowest price the market offers. The order "sell Z" means to sell Z at the highest available market price. The danger with market orders are that they do not limit your exposure to the market. If after you instruct your broker to buy Z, the price of Z skyrockets, you may be faced with paying a lot more than you planned (or than you can).

Fortunately, there are ways to limit your exposure to the market. Specificity helps. One way to control your exposure to the market is through limit orders. Limit orders are instructions to buy at a specific price. They help Barbara to establish floors and ceilings around the purchase price. If, for example, Barbara wishes to buy Z at $5 a share, she may set that price as the ceiling above which she will not buy. Then, if Z trades at $5\frac{1}{8}$ or $5\frac{1}{4}$, Barbara's order will not be executed. Similarly, if Barbara wishes to sell Z, she may set a floor below which she will not sell.

Stop orders, like limit orders, are instructions that help you manage your exposure to the market. The instruction to stop buying Z if it climbs above a certain price is a buy-stop. The instruction to sell Z only so long as it remains above a certain price is a sell-stop.

Limit orders differ from stop orders in that the limit trade may be executed only at a specific price, and no other price, while the stop orders give your broker a range above a floor for selling and a range below a ceiling for buying.

How long is an order valid? Again, it depends on the instructions you give. You may make the order good only for the day on which you place it or a good-till-cancelled or GTC order, which means you have to act to cancel the order when you want your broker's authority to execute the order to terminate.

What Do You Get When You Buy a Security?

What do you get when you buy a security? Well, times have changed. In the not too distant past, stock purchasers were sent the actual certificate of the company, which was the physical evidence of the security. Companies took enormous pride in the appearance of their certificates, and some of the engravings truly were works of art. To trade a security, a purchaser had to deliver the pretty paper to the subsequent buyer or that buyer's representative. If the paper certificate was lost, the consequence could be disastrous.

That is all changed now. Though some companies still do take some pride in the appearance of their certificates, the likelihood that a purchaser will receive one is low in today's market. Today, almost all stock purchases are made through an electronic, paperless system called the "book entry" system. The book entry system reflects trades of securities by making a notation on an electronic ledger. And though purchasers do not get pretty paper, what they get instead is the greatly improved ease of transferring securities.

All this is not to say that securities trades are paperless. Far from it. Following a trade, you will receive a trade confirmation, showing you the number of shares purchased and the purchase price. This information should be retained as part of your permanent files.

Hedging

Hedges protect against movements in price or an adverse change of circumstance. They can be thought of as insurance. Two of the most common hedges are puts and calls.

A put gives you the contractual right to sell the security back to the company. Each put has circumstances under which the put may be exercised. Typically, for example, the put will be exercisable only at a certain "strike price." This strike price limits the company's exposure and locks in your position. For example, Barbara bought 10,000 shares of Z at $5 a share. She also bought a put, entitling her to sell Z to the company for $5. By buying this put, Barbara has limited her losses to the cost of the put and her broker's fees. She will suffer no loss as a result of price movement.

However, the value of the put is affected by market movements. For example, let's assume the cost of the put to Barbara in the above example was $100. This is the value the market has assigned to the right to sell the shares back to the company. Barbara, if she wishes, could sell this right to another Z shareholder, Joan, for the best price she could get. If the market stays where it is, Joan would in all likelihood pay Barbara's minimum asking price of $100.

But what if the market moves? What if Z's share price rises to $7 a share? Now, Barbara would be hard-pressed to find a buyer for her put—no one in his right mind would want to buy the right to sell a share for $5 when he can get $7 in the market. In general, as the share's market price rises above the put's strike price, the value of the put decreases.

And, if the market goes the other way, the value of the put is again affected, only this time the effect is positive. Let's assume again that Barbara bought a put for $100, giving her the right to sell 10,000 shares to the company for $5. If Z's share price falls to $3, Barbara would be sitting pretty. Now, the value of her put is huge. The market value of her 10,000 shares is only $30,000, but the value of the shares at the strike price is $50,000. Thus, her $100 put brings her $20,000 in value.

What, you may ask, determines the initial price for a put? Why was the put initially priced at $200 or $1000? The answer is that the market determines the initial price for a put, and that determination is driven by supply and demand. As for what influences supply and demand, the answer is that the prospects of the company will set the price. If, in our earlier example, we knew that Z's sole product was a herbicide the government had banned as cancer-producing, no one would give a plug nickel for Z's future earnings prospects. Since Z is likely to trade at a price much lower than $5, the value of the put can, again, be huge. So, the market price of the put is likely to be huge. If, on the other hand, we learn that scientists have discovered that Z's herbicide is uniquely effective in fighting off wheat crop damage, Z's share price is likely to rise quite a bit more than $5, and the right to put the shares back to Z at $5 will accordingly be close to zero. Thus, the price of this put is likely to be small or negligible. You may even find it difficult to obtain a quote for such a put.

Warrants are the conceptual opposite of puts. They give you the right to purchase a certain amount of the issuer's stock. The initial price at which the stock can be purchased typically is higher than the market price. Typically, warrants are sold as special rights attached to a bond or other debt security, so you may have trouble finding warrants for a stock you are interested in.

Sometimes small investors think of puts as rather esoteric products. As a result, they shy away from using what can be powerful risk management devices.

Puts and warrants are control vehicles for purchasers. By contrast, calls are control vehicles for issuing companies. A call gives a company the right to buy back securities for a predetermined price. If you are holding a security subject to a call, the value of your security could be diminished since, even more than is usually the case, you cannot count on the income stream from the security throughout its normal term.

Though in the example above, the put was written against the company, it is possible to go out into the market and write a put against other market investors. After all, all your broker has to do is find someone willing to contract to buy back Z shares at a given price. That person does not need to be affiliated with Z. For just as you are seeking to buy a put to protect your portfolio against downside since you fear Z will fall, there are other investors who disagree with your views. They may be looking for a put because they think Z's shares will rise high above $5, and they want the ability to buy your shares at the relatively bargain basement price of $5. But, as a practical matter, our bargain-basement hunter typically would not agree to bind herself to your put because that leaves all the control over timing in your hands. What she really needs is a warrant, entitling her at her option to buy Z for $5 a share.

Stock Exchanges

What do the neighborhood flea market, garage sales, grocery stores, the Moroccan bazaars, and the New York Stock Exchange have in common? They are all marketplaces. And all marketplaces, from the most rudimentary camel post in the Sahara to the most sophisticated, computerized mega-exchange, share a common purpose in life—to provide a central location where buyers and sellers can get together and haggle. There are four major haggle-posts for securities in the United States: The New York Stock Exchange (NYSE), The American Stock Exchange (AMEX), the Commodities Futures Exchange, and the over-the-counter (OTC) market.

Exchanges come in two flavors. First, there is the open-outcry system. If you have ever seen pictures of the action on the floor of the Commodities Futures Exchange, you know what an open-outcry system looks like. It is a circus. A madhouse. Buyers and sellers literally cry out "BUY Z at $5!!" or "SELL Z at 6!!" Your success depends a lot on your strong vocal chords.

Then there are the electronic exchanges. Because these exchanges execute trades on computer screens, they some-times are called "screen-based exchanges." Though elec-tronic exchanges enable the faster processing of orders, you should not get the idea that they are less emotion-packed than open-outcry exchanges. The haggling is just as fierce. Looking at a trading room as key information hits is like watching a tidal wave build. Traders spring into action, shout, and execute orders through the screens, becoming a blur of excitement. In fact, it is almost as close as you will get to watching humans move at the speed of thought.

The NYSE, known in the trade as the "Big Board," is the largest American securities exchange, listing well over 40 billion individual shares of stock and a proportionate num-ber of bonds. The massive, paper-cluttered, trader-packed floor of the Big Board is what people ordinarily think of when they conjure up pictures of the stock market. The amount of dollar value traded on the Big Board is stagger-ing. For example, in 1988, the dollar value of all stocks traded on the exchange was over $1.3 trillion, and the dol-lar value of traded bonds exceeded $7 billion.

You may have wondered how much it costs a company to have its securities traded on the Big Board. Well, the average cost of a seat on the Big Board in 1989 was between $600,000 and $700,000. No small change. And though competition from other exchanges is driving the price down—a seat recently was sold for $350,000—buying a seat on the Big Board still represents a substantial investment for most companies.

The Big Board's operations are governed by the Securities and Exchange Commission as well as by rules the exchange itself sets. These latter rules, sometimes are referred to as "house rules." In the wake of the 1987 Crash, the SEC looked into how each of the major exchange's house rules helped or hurt the effort to stabilize the markets. More on this later.

Trades on the Big Board typically are made in units of 100 shares. A 100-share bundle is called a round lot. Bundles of less than 100 are called odd lots. At IBM's current price of $100 3/8 a share, a round lot would cost over $10,000. Because most smaller investors could not place orders with brokers in the minimum round lot size, a niche has developed for dealers specializing in trading in odd lots. Brokers who are members of the Big Board can sell odd lots to such an odd lot specialist, who in turn will assemble the odd lots into round lots for trading.

The American Stock Exchange is the second largest exchange in the United States. Often it still is referred to as "the Curb," recalling its origins as an open-air market on the curb of the street. In 1988, the Curb traded over 4 billion shares of stock and 600 million bonds. Probably the most frequently asked question about the Curb is how it differs from the New York Stock Exchange. While the Big Board lists most of the largest companies, because of differences in the price of a seat and for other reasons, more small and medium-sized companies list with the Curb. A second reason the Curb is needed is that Big Board rules prohibit a company that lists its stock on the exchange from also listing its options. As a result, often those companies listing stocks on the Big Board will list options on the Curb. And a third difference between the Big Board and the Curb is the cost of a seat. A seat currently averages around $200,000 in contrast to the $600,000 to $700,000 needed to buy a seat on the Big Board.

The third largest exchange in the United States is the over-the-counter or OTC market. The OTC market actually has two parts: (1) the pink sheet market and (2) the National Association of Securities Dealers Automated Quotations System or NASDAQ. Both components of the OTC market are regulated by the NASD.

NASDAQ is a computer screen-based market and has no central trading floor. All information on the stocks traded through the NASDAQ market is centralized on NASDAQ computers in Trumbull, Connecticut. Dealers from all over the country enter the prices at which they are willing to trade into the computers and receive the same information from Trumbull collected from other dealers.

Mutual Funds

Mutual funds are pools of securities managed by fund professionals for a fee.

Because mutual funds have far greater numbers of securities than most investors could amass individually, the funds enable smaller investors to diversify holdings and thus reduce portfolio risk. You buy a share of the total fund, not the individual securities making up the fund's pool.

Mutual funds differ according to their objectives. Though labels change, fund objectives can be arranged from the riskiest equity funds to the most sedate fixed-income bond funds. The concomitant labels will range from "high growth" or "aggressive growth" equities to the "balanced" funds somewhere in the middle of the risk continuum to the relatively low risk "capital preservation" or "bond" or "fixed income" funds. Of course, labels do not make the fund any more than clothes make the man. So, bear in mind that each fund probably has a slightly different view of what separates aggressive from non-aggressive investing, and you must try to look beyond the adjective labels a particular fund uses to discern their strategy and philosophy of investing. How? One place to start is the prospectus. This may come as a surprise, but most investors I know do not read mutual fund prospectuses. Many rely on the advice of brokers to recommend funds, some buy funds based on newspaper or television ads and the like. But there is really only one good way to separate the wheat—meaning well-performing—from the chaff, and that is to do some homework.

While the most careful of you will read the entire prospectus, most of you really are looking only for highlights. If you are only going to read the highlights, here is what you should look for:

Age of the fund. If the fund is less than five years old, you are not going to have enough history to make a reasonably thorough evaluation. Funds in existence fewer than five years should be considered start-ups.

Financial performance over five years. Has the fund outperformed the market over the past five years? Since you are paying a management fee on the assumption that the managers can do better than an unmanaged pool of assets—which is exactly what the S&P 500 measures—there is no reason to pay a fee for managers who have demonstrated they cannot pass this test. A longer history is preferable to a five-year history because it gives you a chance to see how the managers performed in bull and bear markets. Some fund managers do extraordinarily well in bull markets but lack the skills to weather bear markets.

Investment strategies and philosophy. What we mean by strategies and philosophy of investing is not some lofty intellectual ponderings or corporate slogans but the practical inclinations of the fund managers. Do they intend to focus on acquiring stocks of companies with high potential for growth? If so, you can expect that these companies likely will plow back any earnings into development and exploitation of markets rather than paying out dividends to shareholders. Does the fund intend to keep a high cash position? If so, why? Is the fund perhaps guarding against a high number of redemptions? Are the managers likely to plot a well-thought-out course and stick to it—a trait of almost all successful long-term growth fund managers—or are they likely to bolt from a security at the first market jitters? If the fund's performance is tied to a particular individual, a "star," can you count on the star staying for the long term?

Fees. If you buy the fund's shares from a salesperson, you will pay a sales commission, a "load." No-load funds charge no sales commissions. Front-end loads are assessed upon entry into the fund at purchase. Back-end loads are assessed upon exit from the fund at sale. Does this mean that no-load funds charge no fees? No.

All mutual funds, load and no-load, have expenses. These expenses must be covered from sales of the fund shares or from earnings of the funds' securities. There is no other source of income. These expenses include salaries for portfolio managers, traders and researchers, attorney fees, office space, maintaining shareholder records, and marketing expenses, such as printing costs for brochures, prospectuses, quarterly reports, newsletters, and so on.

Fees are either "front-end," meaning you are charged for them when you buy the mutual fund shares or "back-end," meaning you are charged when you sell shares.

Since no-load funds do not charge a front-end or back-end sales commission, they cover these expenses by deducting from dividends they would otherwise pay you. Usually, the fund's managers charge the fund a set percentage of assets under management to cover expenses. For example, Fidelity Magellan, the nation's largest mutual, currently charges an annual management fee of a little less than 1 percent.

Some no-load funds also collect special fees to cover marketing expenses, so-called 12b-1 fees. These 12b-1 fees, named for the SEC rule authorizing them, allow a mutual fund to cover marketing expenses by deducting from your dividends. The funds are required to tell you whether they charge these fees, and you should be especially alert to the existence of such fees. Some funds, aware that 12b-1 charges may not help their image, take care to let you know their charges are "defensive 12b-1" fees. What they mean is that the marketing expenses will be taken from the overall management fee and will not constitute an extra fee on top of the management fee. Of course, the difference may be only academic because it is possible to increase the overall management fee to the point where there is no meaningful distinction between defensive and non-defensive 12b-1s.

Other Sources of Information

You will not find all you need to know about mutual funds in one place. There are, after all, over 2,800 mutual funds in existence today. Fortunately, a number of good books, most priced reasonably, are available:

1. *The Individual Investor's Guide to No-Load Mutual Funds,* Gerril Perritt and L. Ray Shannon. Published in 1985, this is still a good, fairly comprehensive introduction to mutual fund investing.

2. *Kurt Brouwer's Guide to Mutual Funds: How to Invest With the Pros.* Brouwer's book is useful for its clear explanation of the things you should look for in selecting a fund. He gives you a seven-point test and advises you not to buy a fund unless it passes all seven.

3. *Keys to Investing in Mutual Funds,* Warren Boroson. A pocket-sized, unintimidating reference to the field.

4. *The Mutual Fund Encyclopedia,* Gerrald Perritt. Covering over 1000 funds, the book gives returns from 1985 to 1989 (bull market) and from September 1987 to December 1987 (bear market).

Foreign Stocks

Perhaps more than at any time since World War II, Americans feel an interdependence with events happening oceans away. Consider the tumultuous August of 1990. On August 2, Iraq invaded Kuwait. American forces dug in along Kuwait's border with Iraq, and the world was awaiting a showdown between Iraq's president Saddam Hussein and the international forces dedicated to stopping this man whom some tabloids characterized as a modern Hitler. Precipitated by rising oil prices, the stock markets in Tokyo, London, and New York tumbled. Americans began to feel the effects of the crisis in soaring prices at the gas pump. The cost of transporting the military juggernaut of arms and soldiers to the desert was estimated at over $1 billion a month, and President George Bush made an unprecedented appeal to our allies to help foot the bill. Again, we were digesting an international crisis over our morning coffee.

We seem increasingly pulled politically and economically by events around the world. As has been well-documented, television accounts for some of the perception of the strength of that pull.

But television's ability to make us feel connected intimately with Iraq or Tokyo or Panama is not the entire reason we feel the other world's pull. The reality is that we *are* connected. Our lives are connected by trade relationships, cultural identifications, and, yes, ideology. If trade relationships are threatened, our government may feel compelled to act, bridging oceans of distance with a juggernaut of diplomatic and perhaps military machinery funded by our willingness to pay taxes.

And the massive flow of dollars needed to move the juggernaut across national borders are our dollars. *Women's dollars*. Our status as the majority of the workforce and our payroll tax dollars make us, again, a central part of the flow. You are, therefore, in all likelihood an international investor whether you like it or not.

Given our status as international investors, some of us may want to become more skilled at choosing investments for our individual portfolios. And though we cannot always control the selection of countries where our country will invest our collective tax dollars, we can select the countries in the remainder of our international investment portfolio.

Are there reasons other than our *de facto* status as international investors to invest globally? Certainly. The reason is the same one that prompts you to diversify your overall portfolio among several kinds of investment products:

diversification reduces risk. Investing internationally gives you a chance to take advantage of financial opportunities in countries whose economies are growing faster than ours. When America's up, Japan may be down. And when America's down, Japan or Germany may be up. For example, over the last quarter century, Asian equities have increased in value by 16 percent compared to an increase of around 10 percent for New York Stock Exchange listed equities. Diversification also gives you a chance to spread political risk, though this reason is more compelling for those living in countries without long histories of peaceful political transition.

The following section shows you how to invest internationally. We will explore the mechanics of investing in foreign stocks, as well as in mutual funds here and abroad. Not all countries are covered, and the focus mainly is on Western industrialized countries, but the mechanics discussed should generally be applicable to most countries in which you may wish to invest.

Change Brings Opportunity

Change, by and large, is a neutral event. How you react to change, when it comes to investing, is what determines the success you will have. Take, for example, the Iraqi crisis. Not everyone fled from the markets as they began to tumble. Some stayed put. Why? First, not all stocks were falling. Some stocks were doing quite well, with the obvious winners the oil industry stocks. Also, some investors realized that the stock game is a long one, and if they have invested in a well-run company whose business is not harmed materially by the oil crisis, they are better off staying put and waiting for values to stabilize and rise over the long term. In fact, such a crisis can present a rare opportunity to buy at depressed values. Realizing this, some investors were buying *even as the world was on the precipice of war.* They were following the old adage to buy "when there's blood in the streets."

Another change occurring is the dismantling of the Eastern bloc. It may seem incredible to soldiers of World

War II to know that Berlin is once again a single city. The Wall is gone. With these changes have come opportunities to invest in the emerging capitalist democracies of Eastern Europe, in the new amalgam that is the German economy, in an ascendant, unified post-1992 Europe. The scenario calls to mind Japan following World War II. Realizing that a razed Japan had nowhere to go but up, some investors early on put dollars into Japan in whatever form was available. And some investors are flocking to the new European opportunities, hoping for the same results.

How to Buy Foreign Stocks
There are basically three ways to buy foreign stocks:

1. ADRs

2. through an exchange

3. indirectly through one of the many mutual funds predominantly holding foreign securities.

American Depository Receipts or "ADRs" are negotiable certificates representing a certain number of shares of a foreign security. The foreign security itself actually is deposited with an institution in the United States, usually a bank or bank affiliate. ADRs represent some fraction or multiple of the total shares of the foreign security and constitute a depository receipt enabling the holder to transfer title to the corresponding amount of foreign securities simply by transferring the ADRs. Foreign companies may choose to sell their securities through ADRs to save the cost of using an exchange.

Most ADRs are traded through the NASDAQ market. In fact, it has been estimated that twice as many ADRs are traded through NASDAQ as on the New York Stock Exchange and the American Stock Exchange combined.

Sometimes called "American shares," ADRs are the predominant vehicle for the trading of foreign securities in the United States. However, some foreign securities also are traded directly through exchanges. For example, the Sony

Corporation trades its shares through the New York Stock Exchange.

In addition to ADRs and exchange-listed securities, numerous mutual funds invest solely or predominantly in the securities of foreign companies. Almost all of the major mutual funds have "country funds" or "international funds." For example, the Alliance family of funds includes a Spain Fund, a Poland Fund, and a Japan Fund. Fidelity offers a Canada Fund, Europe Fund, Global Bond Fund, International Growth and Income Fund, Overseas Fund, Pacific Basin Fund, Worldwide Fund, and International Opportunities Fund. The proliferation of foreign funds has been a major trend in the mutual fund industry for the past ten years, and all signs are that it is likely to continue.

You should shop for a foreign fund just as carefully as you shop for a domestic one, using the guides discussed earlier.

Finally, you should bear in mind that some domestic funds have significant amounts of their assets invested overseas. If you are already an investor in a mutual fund, you should contact the fund (most large ones have 800 numbers) to find out what percentage of its assets are foreign investments and whether they have a policy of keeping a certain minimum percentage invested overseas. It could be that you are already diversified internationally through a fund you now own.

12. Insurance

The insurance industry has long recognized that men and women present different actuarial risks. As early as 1843, for example, the country's first mutual insurance company, Mutual of New York, charged women a higher premium for life insurance to account for certain "moral hazards" related to increased mortality from child-bearing. Today, because women now tend to outlive men, women are charged lower premiums for life insurance to account for the overall lower rate of mortality. Other types of insurance are also gender-adjusted to account for the different actuarial experience of men and women. Most car insurance premiums, for example, are significantly higher for young males than for women of the same ages.

In this chapter, we review the basic kinds of insurance available and give you a means of determining if and when you need certain policies.

Do All Women Need Life Insurance?

Do all women need life insurance? No, not all women need life insurance. A woman's decision to buy life insurance is a personal choice. First and foremost, her decision depends on how she feels about those she's leaving behind. It also depends on a clear-eyed evaluation of whether, notwithstanding the emotional desire to help surviving loved ones, life insurance is the best vehicle for making such a bequest.

To judge whether you need life insurance, ask yourself, "What is the purpose of life insurance?" Life insurance, despite claims by some life insurance agents to the contrary, is primarily a vehicle for replacement of earnings upon death. The simple job of the life insurance contract is to pay your beneficiaries the face amount of the policy upon your death, provided that you have paid your premiums faithfully. And early life insurance policies did just that, and only that. But today, the simple life insurance contract is not so simple anymore. Though the nature of the beast has not changed—your beneficiaries still are paid upon your death if you have not let the policy lapse—now the beast wears Gucci sneakers. Numerous fancy add-ons have transformed the simple life insurance contract into what some agents would have you believe is a combination surefire wealth builder plus life insurer.

The principal causes of the confusion are various bells and whistles designed to give life insurance the added feature of acting as a means of savings. For this reason, nowadays, people are apt to think of their life insurance policy as an investment in their present net worth. But a life insurance policy really does not add a lot to your present net worth. Instead, what it does—and it does it superbly well—is to improve the size of your death estate. Make no mistake about it—you will not receive much present, living financial benefit other than perhaps a small cash value from your life insurance policy. Your survivors, on the other hand, can reap enormous benefits, depending on the size of your policy.

Thus, the threshold questions you must answer before you sign up for life insurance is, "Will my income be missed?" and if so, "When will it be missed?" Women without children, women with no surviving spouses, women with children and spouses who are self-sufficient, women with significant non-insurance net worth—all of these women might reasonably conclude they do not need life insurance.

And even those women whose earnings might be missed by surviving loved ones ought to ask two additional questions before they buy life insurance: One, would the income replaced by the insurance really be *needed* or would it merely add to what your spouse or kids or whomever could earn on their own? Two, how much does it cost?

Redundancy of coverage costs millions of women and men hundreds of thousands of dollars yearly. Over 120 million Americans carry some form of life insurance. Through our jobs, our spouses, sometimes through our mortgage contracts and other places, we accumulate sometimes overlapping and costly coverage. Before you sign up for life insurance, you should examine any existing policies to avoid double or triple coverage of the same risk. Often, policies limit coverage in cases where you are covered by another policy. As a result, you literally could be paying premiums for nothing.

Who should buy life insurance? As we will discuss more fully below, life insurance is a good buy for those women who

1. feel a responsibility to survivors

2. earn sufficiently high wages or salaries

3. have satisfied themselves that the coverage is not redundant

4. wish to create a large death estate more quickly than they can by saving over the remainder of their life expectancies

5. have no cheaper alternative means of accumulating a sizable bequest

6. after comparing the yearly premium costs with the amount they could accumulate if they invested the premiums in alternative vehicles, have concluded that the insurance available is priced reasonably.

For those women meeting these basic criteria, there are several additional questions to ask before signing up. First, make sure that your policy includes only the add-on features you truly need. Some agents are accustomed to adding certain features automatically when a policy is purchased. Two of the most common involve "waiver-of-premium" and "double indemnity." Because these features can add several percentage points of cost to your annual premiums, it pays, once again to ask, "Why do I need it?" and "How much?"

If the price is right, the waiver-of-premium is generally a good idea. This type of clause provides that if you are disabled, the insurance company will make your life insurance payments for you during your period of disability, so your life insurance policy will not lapse. But be careful about what you are getting with the waiver-of-premium clause. Some people mistakenly believe this clause means the insurance company is insuring them for disability income loss. This is not the case. A waiver of premium clause will not replace income lost during your disability. You will not receive a check from the insurance company during your disability if you elect this clause. You will only have peace of mind that your policy will not lapse during your disability.

The second feature, double indemnity, is better known. This feature doubles or in some cases triples the amount paid to your survivors if you die accidentally. This type of clause may not make sense for you for two reasons. One, you might be buying a multiple of what you really need. For example, if you buy a policy with a face amount of $200,000 because you believe your survivors would need that amount to replace your earnings contribution when you die, why would you buy double or triple this amount through a double indemnity clause? That is, if your survivors really need $400,000 or $600,000, then this is the amount of coverage you should plan on having available from the outset. You should not and can not count on the uncertainty of accidental death to fund a certain need. Two, the double indemnity clause may cost you far more than it is worth in light of the unlikelihood of accidental death.

Double indemnity clauses can add several percentage points a year in premium cost.

Women Breadwinners

Because of the emergence of women as sole or contributing breadwinners in today's two-income families, many women wish to insure their earnings power against such loss. And though in earlier decades a wife's earnings perhaps could be safely viewed as icing on the cake or extra spending cash, today, it may be the wife's salary or wages that means the difference between the family's making the mortgage payment or not, between a child's having enough to go to college or not.

But, curiously, studies that have been made of the way men and women view the importance of insuring a woman's financial contributions to her family show that both men and women tend to value a man's contributions more. And surprisingly, women hold this belief more often than men. A 1981 survey revealed that women believe it is more important to insure a man's life than a woman's, even if the man is not the main breadwinner. When asked whether it is "very important" for a man who contributes to the family income but whose wife outearns him to carry life insurance, 77 percent of women surveyed believed it very important for a man to do so. But when asked whether it is very important for a woman who contributes to the family income but who is outearned by her husband to carry such insurance, only 52 percent of women surveyed believed it was very important to cover the risk of the working wife's death. Likewise, 63 percent of women felt that a couple with double income and no kids (DINKS) should insure the husband, while only 43 percent believed it very important to insure the wife. Thus, it appears that even women sometimes devalue the importance of the financial contributions a woman makes to her family's viability.

Percentage of Women and Men Finding It "Very Important" That Women and Men in Different Situations Carry Life Insurance (1981)

	For Women in *given situation* Responses of:		For Men in *given situation* Responses of:	
	Men %	Women %	Men %	Women %
Single career woman (man) under 30 years old	42	57	46	59
Single career woman (man) over 50 years old	50	63	52	63
Full-time housewife with children under 18	50	61	—	—
Retired woman (man) living with retired spouse	46	55	65	76
Man whose wife also works; Young children at home	—	—	78	87
Contributes to family income; Not main breadwinner	46	52	64	77
Sole support of family	86	92	91	96
Full-time housewife; No children at home	30	34	—	—
Works full-time; Spouse works full-time; No children	40	43	57	63

TABLE 12-1 Source: American Council of Life Insurance

Creating a Big Death Estate Quickly

As we have noted, the one thing life insurance does far better than any other financial product is to help you create a big death estate quickly. Suppose you are a woman at age 50 who is able to save $100 per month and you wish to create the largest death estate possible before your life ends at, say, age 80. You could

1. buy the maximum coverage of life insurance available for $100 per month or

2. invest the $100 in securities or other investments.

Under option one, the life insurance option, the size of your death estate is created immediately upon payment of the first premium. Upon the payment of $100 you now own a death estate equal to $500,000. Subsequent payments merely maintain your right to the death estate. Under any other option, for example, investing in securities, your death estate grows at the investment rate of return, and is largest at the end of the investment period. By contrast, the life insurance option gives you the biggest death estate at the beginning of the investment period. As time goes on and the investment period lengthens, the net cost of creating the death estate grows as you pay more and more premiums to maintain the existence of the death estate.

Because life insurance creates the death estate immediately, and subsequent payments merely maintain the estate, some life insurance analysts refer to life insurance as a "create and save" method of building a death estate, while investing in other products such as securities or bank accounts to build an estate are called "save and create" methods.

In addition to creating a death estate quickly, life insurance proceeds sometimes have special shields from creditors. Several states have "exemption statutes," which protect the proceeds of life insurance from attachment by the creditors of the deceased. A typical exemption statute would direct the proceeds of the policy to the beneficiary, provided the beneficiary is neither the insured nor the insured's estate. Another type of exemption statute directs the proceeds to the beneficiary irrespective of the designation so long as the premium on the policy in question is not greater than a certain maximum, say $1,000.

Types of Life Insurance: Term or Whole

The first known life insurance policy was dated June 18, 1583, and was issued to a William Gybbons for a twelve-month period following the date of issuance. Interestingly, this very first policy resulted in a dispute between the insurance company and the beneficiary. Mr. Gybbons died May 28, 1584, within the calendar year covered by the policy, so upon his death his beneficiary attempted to collect. However, the insurance company refused to pay, claiming that the "twelve-month" period in the insurance contract referred to lunar months, having twenty-eight days, not calendar months, which would mean that Mr. Gybbons died outside the covered period. Fortunately for Gybbons' beneficiaries, the presiding judge viewed the lunar-month argument as, well, lunacy, and the insurance company was ordered to pay.

Policies that, like Gybbons', pay proceeds if death occurs during a certain term are called, aptly enough, "term" insurance. So long as the insured dies within the covered period, the insurance company must pay off. Common periods covered by term insurance are one year, two years, three years, four years, five years, ten years, twenty years, and there also are policies covering you up to age 60 or 65. Policies covering the insured throughout her whole life are called, also aptly, "whole life" policies.

Term insurance policies can be far less costly than whole life policies because of the shorter period covered. For this reason, if you find that you need life insurance, you should determine whether term insurance will suit your needs. You may find many more of such circumstances than you now think. For example, suppose you are a woman who is temporarily supporting her spouse through school. During this period, which may last only four years, it makes little or no sense to take out whole life insurance. Instead, consider taking out a four-year term policy, thereby saving you premium dollars while at the same time meeting your insurance needs. Or suppose you are a woman with children in college. You should consider a term policy for the four-year period during which your earnings contribution would be missed if you die. Beyond that period, your child may very well be able to fend for himself or herself, saving you premium dollars over the cost of whole life.

Under some term insurance policies, the amount of the coverage decreases as the term lengthens. Such policies, called "decreasing term" policies or, if issued as riders, "decreasing term riders," can save you money since premiums are calculated based on the face amount of the policy. These policies or riders make good sense since, as you near the end of the term, your chance of dying within the term decreases, and you therefore need less and less insurance to guard against the risk of death. In contrast, you should note, for whole life insurance, the risk of death increases as you live longer, and therefore there is no similar incentive to reduce the face amount of the whole life policy.

Some insurance companies also offer "increasing term" policies. The coverage of this type of policy increases as you near the end of the term.

Term insurance policies also differ according to whether they are renewable. The basic term insurance policy expires automatically if you are still alive at the end of the period covered. A renewability feature can be advantageous in this respect because at the end of the term, the insurance company must renew at your request. They must renew even if you would, for reasons such as poor health, be otherwise uninsurable at the end of the term. As you would expect, the renewability feature increases the premiums payable under a policy, and again you should weigh the costs in your decision whether to pay for this extra.

Is term life insurance always less expensive than whole life insurance? Yes, if you die within the term. For any given amount of money you have available to invest, you will be able to buy more term insurance than whole life insurance. And if you are sure you are going to die within a certain number of years, term offers the most protection per dollar of any form of insurance. However, if you are alive at the end of the term, a comparison of the costs of term and whole life insurance has a different outcome. Because the whole life insurance has certain cash value upon surrender of the policy, this cash value must be taken into account in determining the true costs of the whole life policy. For example, a leading insurance company provided the annual cost of a five-year term policy (renewable) in the amount of $100,000. You would have to pay $315 for each of the five years of such a policy, which amounts to a total of $1,575 over the five-year term. A level-premium whole life policy from this company would cost you $1054 in annual payments. At the end of five years, you would have paid $5,270. However, the cash surrender value of the whole life policy at the end of five years is $3900, a savings of $205 over the term policy. This analysis ignores the effects of compounded interest payable on the whole life policy, an effect that would further lower the costs of the whole life policy.

Tailoring Your Insurance Plan

As you have seen, term insurance may make more sense for you than whole life for certain periods of your life. And whole life makes sense if you are insuring for longer periods once cash value is taken into account. The key here is to tailor your insurance needs. Do not let a vague, overly broad, albeit well-intentioned desire to provide a security blanket for loved ones drive your decisions about life insurance. In fact, the worst emotion you can bring to bear on the task of evaluating your insurance needs is sentimentality. And you may find that as you tailor your policy or collection of policies to your needs, you will be able to save several percentage points per year in premiums. Over time, these dollars can add up to a savings of thousands of dollars.

Variable Life and Other Bells and Whistles

The first "variable life insurance" policies were written by a Dutch company called DeWaerdye in the 1950s. These early Dutch policies varied in either the amount put in (through premiums) or the amount paid out (through proceeds). Much ballyhooed upon their introduction, these policies were supposed to combine the best of two worlds: providing traditional life insurance protection for the insured while also giving the insured a more high-powered savings vehicle than the more traditional cash value policy.

In the United States, however, the development of variable policies along the Dutch model has been slowed by regulatory impediments. The most prevalent form of variable policy in the United States adjusts the amount of the coverage to the swings of the Consumer Price Index or some other cost-of-living index, not in accordance with the performance of selected equities. The policyholder pays an extra rider amount annually depending on the movement of the index.

The principle of adjusting your life insurance coverage to swings in the cost-of-living makes some sense. Since life insurance coverage is intended to replace earnings power of the insured, and since that earnings power is eroded or enhanced as the cost-of-living swings, it makes sense to have the adjustment. However, the issue boils down to a matter of cost. Not all companies offer the added protection against swings in inflation and other costs at an affordable price. Here, as with other products, comparison shopping is indispensable.

Should You Insure Your Kids?

Should you insure your kids? The answer in most cases is no. Unless you're the parent of an income-earning child (a tennis star, a child actress, an extraordinarily successful lemonade stand operator), the child has no income the loss of which insurance could replace. In the meantime, you would be paying premiums for nothing. Many people who take out insurance on their kids do so because of that

vague desire to provide a security blanket we have identified earlier. Indeed, they may even mistakenly believe they
are somehow protecting the child. In fact, one woman
interviewed for this chapter said she believed she was taking out children's insurance "for college costs." But, as you
can see, this type of life insurance will not protect your
child financially. And even if the policy has some minuscule cash value by the time your child reaches 18, you
would be much better off putting the money you would
otherwise spend on premiums directly into a savings plan
for your child.

Between You and Your Husband

Policies taken out by your husband to provide for you
and the kids after he is gone typically are only in his name.
Often little thought is given as to who should own the
policy. But, as we briefly mentioned in Chapter 3, it makes
a great deal of sense to have these policies put in both
your names. "Ownership" of a life insurance policy gives
the owner certain rights exercisable during the life of the
insured. Though policies differ, these ownership rights
typically include:

1. the right to designate the beneficiary

2. the right to take out loans against the policy or use the
   policy for other collateral purposes

3. the right to surrender the policy for cash value

As joint owner of the policy insuring your husband, you
and he could choose to allow him to use the policy for collateral purposes, if he wishes, while leaving the death benefit untouched for you and the kids. Or you could use the
policy for collateral purposes and still retain the death benefits. You should investigate whether your current policy
would permit such a joint arrangement, and if it does not,
consider switching to one that does.

Another issue you and your husband should handle is setting up a procedure to prevent missed payments. Under some policies, the insurance company can notify a third party in the event a payment is missed or is late. The third party then is able to make the payment and avoid lapse. Again, it is worth your while to consider setting up a missed-payment procedure to avoid losing benefits.

Widowhood

Until recently, most women dealt with life insurance only in their capacity as widows. And, because women continue to outlive men, studies show that as many as eight out of every ten married women will one day be widows. In preparation for the day when you may have to deal with the details of your husband's life insurance, there are a few steps you should take now. One, make sure you know where your husband's policies are kept. If he is keeping them in his safe deposit box, have them transferred to another place over which you have joint control. In the event of his death, most states would require that a state official be present for the opening of a safe deposit box in his name alone. Keeping the policy in a safe deposit box would only mean delays and hassles during a time when you may not be emotionally fit to handle them. Two, take the time, now, to understand what is in the policies. Do they cover burial costs? What paperwork must you furnish before pay-out? Is the pay-out in a lump sum or in installments? Handling these types of issues before death occurs makes good financial and emotional sense.

Disability Insurance

Earlier we noted that many people mistakenly believe that waiver-of-premium clauses in life insurance policies protect against loss of income during disability. For those of you who feel you need disability insurance, such protection should be purchased as a separate policy or separate clause in a comprehensive life/disability policy. Whether purchased separately or as part of an umbrella policy, disability insurance should be evaluated in terms of whether it would furnish sufficient replacement income and, as always, whether it costs too much for what it provides.

When do you need disability insurance? As with life insurance, you should pinpoint those periods in your life when your income would be missed. But unlike with life insurance, you should also pinpoint how much income you yourself would need to cover your living expenses. Bear in mind in making this determination that many people underestimate the amount of replacement income they would need because they fail to take into account potential extra costs during disability, such as nursing care. As a result, you should estimate your replacement income as somewhat higher than the amount you are earning. Also, because as a woman you are more likely than a man to provide a host of household caretaking services, services that would have to be purchased (if not replaced by family and friends pitching in), your estimate also should account for this loss—if the extra premium cost is not too high.

When you calculate the amount of disability coverage you need, do not forget to take into account government benefits you may be entitled to receive. Remember, Social Security is both a retirement plan and a health care/disability insurance plan. You have already paid for these features through FICA payroll deductions. If you become disabled and have paid FICA taxes, you are entitled to receive benefits regardless of your age at the onset of disability. Your spouse may also be entitled to receive benefits (regardless of age) if he is caring for your child and the child is under 16 years of age or if the child being cared for is disabled. And your child may be entitled to receive benefits if he or she is under 18 (or under 19 if the child is still in high school). If your child is disabled, he or she can receive benefits regardless of age. In addition to Social Security, which is a federal benefit, some states also have "state cash sickness programs." Currently, California, Hawaii, New Jersey, New York, and Rhode Island have some form of sickness program. Check with your particular state government if you live in one of these states to ascertain the requirements you would have to meet to qualify for benefits. Though rules vary, basically the state benefit is a percentage of your average weekly earnings up to a set maximum. For example, you could be paid 50 percent of your weekly earnings up to a maximum of $135 per week. The coverage period generally is short. Most states cut off benefits after twenty-six weeks of disability, though California covers its residents for fifty-two weeks.

The important thing to remember is that you ought not to buy more than you truly need. Price each add-on feature separately to determine whether the increased cost of the extra coverage is unreasonable. Comparison shopping among insurance companies will help you to improve the deal you get for the price of disability insurance—or any other insurance for that matter.

How to Use Life Insurance for Pension Maximization—A Woman's Special Edge

Because women outlive men, we face a greater risk of outliving our retirement dollars. The risk is compounded by the fact that women lag men in lifetime earnings, and since lower lifetime earnings as a general matter mean lower Social Security as well as private pension benefits, women tend to have fewer resources than men during their golden years. Yes, for those women who have been smart or lucky enough to follow a well-planned investment strategy earlier in life, the financial disparity is lessened. But what if you are one of the many women who have no such plan and are nearing retirement? Is there any solution for you?

Fortunately, there is a little-known solution that turns the fact that you will tend to outlive men from a financial disadvantage to an advantage. Called pension maximization, or "pension Max," it works like this. If you are covered by a retirement annuity plan and you are married, you must by law give your spouse survivor rights in your plan. However, when the time for retirement nears, you will be asked to select among a number of options for paying out these annuity benefits. The options can be complex, but basically they boil down to:

1. receiving a monthly check for the remainder of your life, called a single life annuity

2. receiving a smaller check each month but also having your spouse covered for the remainder of his life after you die, called a joint and survivor annuity.

It occurred to pension planners that if they combined annuity pensions with life insurance, some married couples, in theory at least, could have their cake and eat it too. The strategy would have the couples select the single life annuity option, and thereby get the higher monthly annuity check, and buy a life insurance policy to cover the possibility that the annuitant-spouse would die before the uncovered spouse. The life insurance policy would be purchased as near to retirement time as possible to keep the total amount of out-of-pocket premiums the couple would pay through their retirement years as low as possible.

Theory is beautiful. But in practice, it turns out that the numbers do not work for all but the rare cases where the husband is not the annuitant because the cost of life insurance for a man near retirement age is far too high to make it feasible.

But for a woman in good health, the numbers do work out. This is so because a woman in good health, even one near retirement age, still has enough years of life ahead of her to make life insurance policy premiums affordable. As a result, the life insurance premiums, subtracted from the higher single life annuity monthly checks, still leave far more annuity than the couple would get by electing the joint and survivor option. In this case it can pay handsomely for being a woman. "The female employee can play the arbitrage," observes Ethan Kra of the benefits consulting firm, William M. Mercer, Inc.

There are risks to this strategy, however. One, the insurance policy may not pay as much as you counted on, especially if the pay-out is based on investment performance. Two, inflation, as we have seen, erodes the value of the life insurance pay-out. At a 4 percent inflation rate, for example, the policy proceeds would lose half their value in eighteen years, so your spouse may end up with less than he needs to get by. And three, someone may make a mistake and let the policy lapse.

Health Insurance

Though not all women need life insurance, we all do need health insurance. The number and variety of health insurance products have increased dramatically over the past twenty years. Today, women may choose from a broad range of healthcare products and services, including traditional major medical plans such as Blue Cross/Blue Shield, health care maintenance organization (HMO) plans, and various other group plans.

The total costs you pay for your health insurance plan can vary greatly, depending on the option. As a general rule, the tradeoff is between lower premiums and less flexibility in selection of care professionals or higher premiums and greater flexibility in selection of such professionals. For example, under your Blue Cross/Blue Shield plan you may pay higher premiums than through an HMO, but you can go to any doctor you choose. On the other hand, if you are satisfied with the doctors designated under an alternative HMO plan, you can save thousands of premium dollars by selecting this option.

The costs you pay also depend to some extent on the plan's source. Group health care plans available through your employer typically are less costly than plans you purchase individually.

A hidden health cost many women bear results from coverage redundancy. If you are a married working woman covered under a group plan through your job, you should also explore whether it is cheaper to drop your coverage and be added to your husband's group plan. Some states even have laws entitling you to continue your coverage for a certain period, usually two years (though perhaps at a slightly higher premium) even if your spouse is terminated. Or you may find it less expensive to carry your husband on your group plan, saving your household the premiums he would otherwise pay to his group insurer.

Car Insurance

You need two types of car insurance: insurance to cover damage to your car or to another car involved in an accident and liability insurance to cover personal injuries to yourself or others.

You may be surprised to know that you obtain car insurance as an add-on benefit automatically when you use certain credit cards to rent a car. Cars rented with certain gold credit cards, for example, automatically carry collision damage. Personal (as opposed to business) and small corporate American Express card accounts automatically insure against damage to a rental car. But to take advantage of this cost savings, you must decline the option to buy this insurance on the car rental agreement.

The biggest potential cost you face if you are involved in a car accident is personal injury damage. If someone is seriously hurt or killed, the damage could range into many millions of dollars, so make sure that whatever policy or combination of policies you select, you are covered against this risk.

13. How to Get There from Here

The previous chapters will help you learn to evaluate your financial needs and match those needs with suitable investment products. And the strategies for saving and budgeting—self-bills, mad money accounts, acquiring the haggling habit, using automatic account builders and so on—can help you begin to accumulate sufficient funds to buy the products you select. But what the previous chapters cannot help you do is take the most important step of all—the first step. They cannot make you begin. Only you can do that.

Some of us are born self-motivated. We wake up without alarm clocks, leap out of bed in the morning, free of doubts, ready to tackle whatever. We make lists and, to the disgust of our fellow human beings, accomplish each task on the lists by the end of the day. We are either blessed or miscreant, depending on your point of view.

Most of us, however, are not self-starters. We hesitate, procrastinate, plan to do and plan some more but somehow never get to all of it. Some of us never get around to any of it. For the majority of us, then, nothing gets done without a jump starter. In view of that reality, I offer the following.

There are really only two words you need to get on your way to creating the portfolio you would like to have. The first word is simple. It can be used as a wedge to create a little more budget space. The word is "no."

During your day, you probably encounter at least five instances in which saying "no" would prevent dollars from flying out of your purse and into the pockets of someone else. Here is an example. My husband and I took private ballroom dance lessons from a well-known studio. Eleven lessons, $600 dollars. At the end of lesson seven, our instructor, let's call her Georgina, began to prime us for the inevitable sales pitch designed to snare us for an additional year or more. "Only $3,000 for a lifetime of enjoyment," she crooned. "A pitifully small investment in yourself."

We said "no." And in doing so, saved ourselves $3,000. What we gave up was the special attention you get in private lessons. Instead, we enrolled in cheaper group classes at the Y, and, more or less, did not miss a beat. That's an easy one. What about requests from family for loans, co-workers for favorite causes, schools for alumni gifts? How do you say "no" to these requests? It's tougher. But if you have decided on an investment plan, one that truly meets your needs, and there is no more to give, you have got to find a way to become comfortable saying "no." And though the goal is not to say "no" to all these requests, you must learn to turn down those that keep you from funding your own lifetime needs. The solution involves practice, as much practice as you need to overcome the financially self-destructive habit of giving more than you truly have.

To paraphrase an old song, there must be fifty ways to say "no." Here are a few:

1. "That sounds very worthwhile. It sounds like just the kind of thing I'd love to contribute to, and I will contribute. But unfortunately, my own financial circumstances don't permit me to make the full contribution. I'm sure you can appreciate that. But because I'd like to show my support, I'm willing to give you $ _____. Hope it helps. Good luck."

2. Try a variation of 1. if you want to give services, not money. "That sounds very worthwhile. It sounds like just the kind of thing I'd love to contribute to, and I will contribute. But not financially. I'm pretty good at writing

fund-raising letters (stuffing envelopes, cold-calling, etc.). Let me draft one for you as my contribution."

3. "I'm sorry to hear that. It always hurts me to hear you're in need. Listen, not to bring up the past, but did that loan I made you last year help you out any? I remember last year when you needed that loan, I reached deep down into the budget and, to tell you the truth, I still haven't recovered financially. Can you understand that? Anyway, I don't want to let you down completely but I just can't find the extra money right now."

4. "Does the boss really want us all to contribute? By payroll deduction? Wow, that's going to be tough for me this year. I'd love to give, but I just don't think I'll be able to this year. Besides, I think my husband gives through his job."

5. "Yes, I know it looks just like it was built for me. Yes, I like to live a little—who doesn't. But that price. . . . Listen, I think I'll pass on this for now. I may be willing to buy in a month or so, but right now I think that's a little rich for my blood, you know what I mean?"

Once you have gotten the hang of saying "no," there is another word you have got to master to right your financial ship. That word is "self-permission." Why is self-permission so essential? The idea of "permission" is central to what it means to be a girl or a woman in our culture. Since the time we were girls, we have been socialized as nurturers and pleasers. Little girls, according to many sociologists, are taught to value themselves according to their ability to be resources to others while little boys are taught to acquire resources. As women, we have come to believe, perhaps not surprisingly, that being a good resource—a good resource to your husband as his wife, a good resource to your children as their mother, a good resource as daughter to an elderly parent and so on—is about the highest aspiration a human being can have. And of course in many ways the magnanimity and beneficence of the nurturer are wonderful qualities. Trouble is, this lifelong habit of being a good resource develops in many women a deep need to be needed, irrespective of whether the person being helped is supportive or abusive, irrespective of whether the help truly is needed. We become the world's best pleasers.

When we try to learn to assess our separate needs, such as our need to meet the special financial risks women face, our socialization as pleasers becomes an obstacle. It blocks our path because competing needs will always seem more important than our personal needs. The Good Girl, remember, never "thinks of self."

The only way around this obstacle is to give ourselves permission to do what we have to do. We must give ourselves permission to leave the duties of pleasing others for just long enough to take care of ourselves. In effect, we must learn to give ourselves permission to please ourselves. Self-permission, after a while, will begin to feel acceptable. And I do not think we need to worry about the pendulum swinging all the way to the other side: We will not become so self-focused that we neglect those worthy of our time and energy. There is little risk of this ounce of self-permission outweighing a lifetime of indoctrination in the other direction. Instead, what will happen is that we will begin to achieve more of a balance between pleasing all others and pleasing ourselves. Yes, we will continue to need to be needed. But some of those needs we will fulfill, finally, will be ours.

To some of you, there is no financial conflict between meeting the needs of others and your personal needs. You either have more money than you need to do both or you have reconciled the conflict by deciding how much you can do and resolving not to try to do more than that. You are lucky. But for many more, this reconciliation, even after putting down this book, will be painful. It may make you despair. It may make you mad. In any event, try to remember that the many years of neglect that brought you to the point where you are today cannot be reversed in a day. It will take time. It will take patience. Give yourself a little of both. And while you're at it, forgive yourself for not starting sooner.

Appendix A

The Risk Questionnaire

If you know the right questions to ask, you can create your own investment profile. What follows is an extensive questionnaire designed to help you identify your current assets and to place them into proper risk categories. Do not be daunted by the length of the list. Try to clear away an hour free of distractions to complete the questionnaire. For some of you it may take a few sessions.

The overview explains the meanings of various categories of assets, followed by the questionnaire. The overview is general, and if after reading the overview you are still unclear about the definitions of some of the products, flip over to the index to locate the chapter dealing with the product.

Overview to What Certain Categories Mean

Each of the eight categories of assets in the Risk Profile Questionnaire has different inherent risks.

For example, category (a), "cash," has no payment risk. If you own cash in any form listed in (a), you can be as sure as possible that you will receive your full dollar value back. We have included only bank accounts (or certificates of deposit) up to $100,000 per bank. The reason is that under federal government deposit insurance rules, discussed in more detail in Chapter 9, only up to $100,000 per individual account is insured at an institution. Any amounts you have in a bank or savings and loan above these amounts fall into the category of what I call "near-cash," meaning there is some risk that you will not receive full payment on demand or maturity. The bottom line is that if you have more than $100,000 parked in a single bank, the excess amount is not, within our definition, cash. Instead, all you own is a possibility of payment.

Categories (c) and (d) distinguish between investment grade bonds and other debt obligations and non-investment grade products. These obligations are the issuing corporation's or entity's IOU, its promise to repay the obligation in full according to the stated terms. As an investor in these products, you are in effect a lender, and the issuer is your debtor. In Chapter 11, the strategies you should use to evaluate these products are explored, but for now, we need only discuss the difference between "investment grade" debt paper and below investment grade paper. Debt paper is "investment grade" if it has been rated in one of the top five categories (AAA through BBB–) by a nationally recognized ratings agency. The lowest category into which a product may fall and still be considered investment grade is BBB–. Lower categories (BB–, CCC, CC, etc.) are considered "below investment grade" or "speculative."

Blue-chip stocks and other high-grade equities are an important category of assets for almost all investors. Blue-chippers are stocks of companies that have for years performed well, producing good rates of return, year-in and year-out. They are marked by stability of performance and, often, management. Watching a blue-chipper perform over the years can be as dull as watching water boil, but it can also be very profitable. The Dow Jones Industrial Average (DJIA) is an index of the stock of thirty large industrial companies typically regarded as blue-chippers. These companies are almost all household names: General Motors, IBM, McDonnell-Douglas, Weyerhauser, and so on. Other blue-chip stocks can be found among the 50 companies making up the bundle of stocks tracked by the S&P 500. The S&P 500 includes stocks of service industries, such as McDonalds, as well as industrial stocks. Though there is no uniform standard used to measure the performance of blue-chip stocks, certain benchmarks typically are used. Often, blue-chippers are said to be performing as expected if, over a ten- to twenty-year period, they achieve a rate of return of at least 10 percent. For all other equities, the performance measured in rates of return has been spotty. As Professors Fischer and Lorie of the University of Chicago's Graduate School of Business report in their book, *A Half Century of Returns on Stocks and Bonds*, some stocks, over the fifty-year period ending in 1976, became worthless while others increased in value hundredsfold. For the period between 1980 and 1990, the stock market (as measured by the S&P 500) experienced spectacular growth:

$$
\begin{array}{rl}
1980 & - \quad 32.27\% \\
1981 & - \quad -5.01 \\
1982 & - \quad 21.44 \\
1983 & - \quad 22.56 \\
1984 & - \quad\; 6.10 \\
1985 & - \quad 31.57 \\
1986 & - \quad 18.56 \\
1987 & - \quad\; 5.10 \\
1988 & - \quad 16.61 \\
1989 & - \quad 31.69 \\
1990 & - \quad -4.5 \text{ (estimate)}
\end{array}
$$

What a decade. But not all decades will duplicate the performance of the Roarin' Eighties. What you must do, again, is to decide what percentage of your portfolio should be devoted to blue-chip stocks. That decision will depend on a lot of factors, including the condition of your nerves.

According to Census Bureau data, the richer you are, the more likely you are to own stocks and mutual fund shares. Of those earning over $4,000 per month, stocks and mutual fund shares make up an average of over 64 percent of their net worth, while the percentage is only slightly over 24 percent for those earning monthly incomes of between $2,000 and $3,000, and only 8 percent for those earning between $900 and $1,999 monthly.

Real estate makes up the next asset category. Americans depend on home equity for the largest share of their net worth, with over two-thirds of all households reporting that home equity accounts for 41 percent of their net worth. The median value of equity in American households is approximately $41,000.

Because the remaining asset categories mean what you would ordinarily expect them to mean, let's proceed to the questionnaire.

RISK PROFILE QUESTIONNAIRE

1. Age _____
2. Current assets

   a. Cash
      i. Cash on hand in federally insured bank savings and loan accounts (checking, saving, money market accounts, etc.) up to $100,000
      ii. Certificates of deposit in federally insured banks up to $100,000
      iii. Cash on your person or in your home

   b. Near-Cash
      i. Cash on hand in bank or savings and loan accounts (checking, saving, money market accounts) exceeding $100,000
      ii. Cash in bank certificates of deposit exceeding $100,000
      iii. All cash in money market funds (these are funds maintained in non-bank institutions)
      iv. All cash in credit union accounts
      v. Cash value of United States Treasury bills, notes, or bonds

    c. Investment Grade Debt Paper.
- i. Market value of corporate bonds rated AAA, AAa, AA, aa2, A, BBB or BB by a nationally recognized ratings agency such as Standard & Poors Corporation (S&P) or Moody's Investors Services Inc. (Moody's), Duff & Phelps, or Fitch's Investor's Service
- ii. Market value of commercial paper (maturity less than 270 days) rated by a nationally recognized ratings agency A-1 or P-1
- iii. Collateralized mortgage obligations (CMOs) rated AAA if you own one of the two products having the shortest maturities.
- iv. Eighty percent of the outstanding principal amount of mortgages which you, as lender, have extended, if such mortgages are fully secured by real estate with stable or appreciating market value
- v. Asset-backed securities structured as debt, rated AAA, with fully-amortized principal payment schedules (as opposed to so-called "bullet" or balloon principal payment structures) and at least semi-annual interest payment schedules
- vi. Municipal (city, state) bonds rated B or higher by a nationally recognized ratings agency

    d. Below Investment Grade Debt Paper
- i. Any corporate bonds not included in (c)
- ii. Any commercial paper not included in (c)
- iii. Any municipal securities not included in (c)
- iv. Any mortgages, CMOs, asset-backed securities or other bonds (including high-yield "junk" bonds)

   e. Blue-Chip Stocks and Other High Quality Equities

      i. Common, voting (usually class B) stock of the 30 corporations listed in the Dow Jones Industrial Average or of corporations which have achieved a 10 percent rate of return on equity for fifteen out of the past twenty years

     ii. Mortgage-backed pass-through securities guaranteed by the United States (such as the Government National Mortgage Association, known as "Ginnie Mae") or an agency or instrumentality of the United States (such as the Federal National Mortgage Association, known as "Fannie Mae," or the Federal Home Loan Mortgage Association, known as "Freddie Mac")

    iii. Shares of mutual funds rated among the top ten funds in the annual Lipper Growth Fund Index or the Lipper Average for Growth Funds

    iv. Shares of mutual funds that have returned an average of over 11 percent per annum and have been rated among the top five funds over the past twenty years in surveys conducted by *Money Magazine, Fortune, Forbes,* or as reported by *The Wall Street Journal, Barron's,* or *The New York Times*

     v. Stocks of foreign corporations that have been in existence for at least fifteen years and which, over the past fifteen years, have achieved an average rate of return of at least 11 percent

  f. Other Equities

      i. All common stocks not included in (e)

     ii. All mutual fund shares or pass-through equities not included in (e)

g. Real Estate
   i. The market value of real estate used as your primary residence
   ii. Ninety percent of the market value of real estate generating positive rental income before taxes are considered
   iii. Ninety percent of the market value of limited partnership interests in real estate partnerships

h. Jewelry and Collectibles
   i. The market value of mint comic books as determined by Overstreet's price guide
   ii. The market value of baseball cards as determined by Overstreet's Price Guide
   iii. One hundred percent of the pawn shop value of all rings, bracelets, necklaces, or other jewelry or 80 percent of the appraised value for insurance purposes
   iv. The market value of antiques and rare dining or decorative plates, silverware, and crystal

i. Clothes
   i. Fifty percent of the lesser of the purchase price or the insurable value of all genuine fur coats
   ii. Ten percent of the purchase price or the insurable value of all other clothing

Appendix B

Filling out a ledger like this each month will make it easier for you to keep track of your expenses and income. This in turn will let you see where changes can be made. The following ledger covers three months to help you get an idea of your average monthly income and expenditures.

MONTHLY HOUSEHOLD LEDGER

DATE

Opening Balance as of _____

$ _____

I. Additions

Checking $ _____

$_____

$_____

$_____

$_____

Savings (operational) $_____

    $_____

    $_____

    $_____

    $_____

CD   (Maturity Date)

    $_____   _____

    $_____   _____

    $_____   _____

    $_____   _____

Other (specify) $_____

    $_____

    $_____

    $_____

    $_____

II. Expenses $_____
                           date written

Rent $_____

Food $_____

Trans. $_____

Laundry $_____

Grooming $ _____

Misc. $ _____

Gifts (specify purpose)

    $_____   For   _____

    $_____   For   _____

    $_____   For   _____

    $_____   For   _____

Check(s) written for this period
(indicate purpose)

1. $_____   Purpose   _____

2. $_____   Purpose   _____

3. $_____   Purpose   _____

4. $_____   Purpose   _____

5. $_____   Purpose   _____

6. $_____   Purpose   _____

7. $_____   Purpose   _____

8. $_____   Purpose   _____

9. $_____   Purpose   _____

10. $_____   Purpose   _____

Cash machine withdrawals from ATM's
(indicate purpose)

1. $ _____   Purpose _____

2. $ _____   Purpose _____

3. $ _____   Purpose _____

4. $ _____   Purpose _____

5. $ _____   Purpose _____

6. $ _____   Purpose _____

7. $ _____   Purpose _____

8. $ _____   Purpose _____

9. $ _____   Purpose _____

10. $ _____   Purpose _____

Total opening balances $_____

Minus total expenses $_____

                            $_____

Comments or questions _____

_____

Signature_____

Signature_____

MONTHLY HOUSEHOLD LEDGER

DATE

Opening Balance as of _____

$_____

I. Additions

   Checking $_____

      $_____

      $_____

      $_____

      $_____

   Savings (operational) $_____

      $_____

      $_____

      $_____

      $_____

   CD   (Maturity Date)

      $_____   _____

      $_____   _____

      $_____   _____

      $_____   _____

Other (specify) $_____

    $_____

    $_____

    $_____

    $_____

II. Expenses $_____
                           date written

Rent $ _____

Food $ _____

Trans. $ _____

Laundry $ _____

Grooming $ _____

Misc. $ _____

Gifts (specify purpose)

    $_____   For   _____

    $_____   For   _____

    $_____   For   _____

    $_____   For   _____

Check(s) written for this period
(indicate purpose)

1. $_____   Purpose   _____

2. $_____   Purpose   _____

3. $_____   Purpose   _____

4. $_____   Purpose   _____

5. $_____   Purpose   _____

6. $_____   Purpose   _____

7. $_____   Purpose   _____

8. $_____   Purpose   _____

9. $_____   Purpose   _____

10. $_____   Purpose   _____

Cash machine withdrawals from ATM's
(indicate purpose)

1. $_____   Purpose   _____

2. $_____   Purpose   _____

3. $_____   Purpose   _____

4. $_____   Purpose   _____

5. $_____   Purpose   _____

6. $_____   Purpose   _____

7. $_____   Purpose   _____

8. $ _____   Purpose _____

9. $ _____   Purpose _____

10. $ _____   Purpose _____

Total opening balances $_____

Minus total expenses $_____

                           $_____

Comments or questions _____

_____

Signature_____

Signature_____

MONTHLY HOUSEHOLD LEDGER

DATE

Opening Balance as of _____

$ _____

I. Additions

   Checking $ _____

      $ _____

      $ _____

      $ _____

      $ _____

   Savings (operational) $ _____

      $ _____

      $ _____

      $ _____

      $ _____

   CD   (Maturity Date)

      $ _____   _____

      $ _____   _____

      $ _____   _____

      $ _____   _____

Other (specify) $_____

    $_____

    $_____

    $_____

    $_____

II. Expenses $_____
                       date written

Rent $ _____

Food $ _____

Trans. $ _____

Laundry $ _____

Grooming $ _____

Misc. $ _____

Gifts (specify purpose)

    $_____   For _____

    $_____   For _____

    $_____   For _____

    $_____   For _____

Check(s) written for this period
(indicate purpose)

1. $_____   Purpose   _____

2. $_____   Purpose   _____

3. $_____   Purpose   _____

4. $_____   Purpose   _____

5. $_____   Purpose   _____

6. $_____   Purpose   _____

7. $_____   Purpose   _____

8. $_____   Purpose   _____

9. $_____   Purpose   _____

10. $_____   Purpose   _____

Cash machine withdrawals from ATM's
(indicate purpose)

1. $_____   Purpose   _____

2. $_____   Purpose   _____

3. $_____   Purpose   _____

4. $_____   Purpose   _____

5. $_____   Purpose   _____

6. $_____   Purpose   _____

7. $_____   Purpose   _____

8. $ _____   Purpose _____

9. $ _____   Purpose _____

10. $ _____   Purpose _____

Total opening balances $_____

Minus total expenses $_____

                           $_____

Comments or questions _____

_____

Signature_____

Signature_____

Index